GETTING YOURS

IT'S NOT TOO LATE TO HAVE THE WEALTH YOU WANT

Bambi Holzer

With Elaine Floyd

JOHN WILEY & SONS, INC.

Published by John Wiley & Sons, Inc., New York.

Published simultaneously in Canada.

This publication is designed to provide accurate and authoritative information in regard to the subject matter covered. It is sold with the understanding that the publisher is not engaged in rendering professional services. If professional advice or other expert assistance is required, the services of a competent professional person should be sought.

Library of Congress Cataloging-in-Publication Data:

Holzer, Bambi.
    Getting yours : it's not too late to have the wealth you want / by Bambi Holzer with Elaine Floyd.
       p. cm.
    Includes index.
    ISBN 0-471-41127-2 (cloth : alk. paper)
      1. Finance, Personal—United States. 2. Investments—United States. 3. Wealth—United States. I. Floyd, Elaine, 1961– II. Title.

  HG179.H5948 2001
  332.024'01—dc21   2001026752

Printed in the United States of America.

10 9 8 7 6 5 4 3 2 1

To my patient, supportive, loving husband Charles Schatz, M.D. You made my life complete by sharing Danny, Jon (may he rest in peace), and Ali with me, who, along with Steve, brought sheer joy into my world in Madison and J.T.

B. H.

ACKNOWLEDGMENTS

This book was made possible by the expertise and tireless efforts of many people.

My management team at A.G. Edwards, John Lee and Frank Bennett. Also, my corporate communications folk: Debbie Geringer, Margaret Welch, and Teresa Coll.

My dedicated assistants: Jenny Brearton, Michael Lutz, and Jennifer Hiller. You guys are the greatest.

The team at John Wiley & Sons: Joan O'Neil, Debby Englander, Greg Friedman, Peter Knapp, and Mary Daniello. Also, my publicist in New York, Dick Wolfe.

My wonderful friends and clients who shared their ideas and stories and helped mold this book: Barry Breslow, Larry Friedman, Larry Kopald, Herb Lawrence, Vicky Malone, Robert Rosenbloom, Lou Rosenmayer, Steve Rosin, and Brad Salter, Ph.D.

My very supportive family: my mother Estelle and her husband Jack Shore; my sister Audrey, her husband E. Leonard Rubin, and my nieces Margot and Bette; and my amazing husband, Charles, and my family who make it all worthwhile: Danny, Ali, and Steve, and my darlings Madison and J.T.

B. H.

CONTENTS

CHAPTER ONE

THE NATIONAL LAMENT

Everyone Is Getting Rich but Me

Everyone imagined that the passion for tulips would last for ever, and that the wealthy from every part of the world would send to Holland, and pay whatever prices were asked for them.

Men, it has been well said, think in herds; it will be seen that they go mad in herds, while they only recover their senses slowly, and one by one.

Extraordinary Popular Delusions
and the Madness of Crowds
Charles MacKay

IF IT WEREN'T SO SAD, it would be easy to say that some greedy people got what they deserved. In the latest mania that consumed investors at the dawn of the third millennium, people learned the hard way that dumping their life savings into risky stocks—and going into debt to do it—was not the sure road to riches. Some ended up worse off than others. Those who mortgaged their homes and maxed out their credit cards to buy stocks on margin not only lost everything they had, but they also wound up deep in debt with little to show for it except a tax write-off and a lesson they will never forget. (Fortunately these were not my clients but people I've met in various travels.) Those who took my advice and risked just a small portion of their money came crawling back, deeply appreciative of my warnings and thankful that the rest of their portfolio was doing fine.

I never say "I told you so," because I understand how easy it can be to succumb to the temptations of the markets. After 20 years as a financial advisor I know as well as anyone that the lure of the markets and the prospect of extraordinary riches can be enormously compelling, especially when it all seems so easy. You don't have to work very hard. You don't have to be especially smart. You don't have to be born into the right family or have superhuman gifts. All you have to do is pay attention to the markets, pick the right stocks, and voila! You're rich. It happened to the thousands of people who invested early in Microsoft or Dell Computer and held on to their stock throughout the 1990s. It happened to the lucky people who got in and out of stocks like Qualcomm or Amazon.com at just the right time in these stocks' recent, but extraordinarily volatile, trading histories. It happened to people who went to work for brand-new companies with funny-sounding names like Yahoo! and who took stock options in lieu of high salaries because they believed the company was onto something big—and who cashed in early, before the stock fell 90 percent from its high.

As the 20th century came to a close, everyone seemed to be saying, "If all these people can get rich the quick and easy way, why can't I?" And so we saw investors doing some very strange things in their quest for extraordinary wealth. One client who had known me since childhood and who had been investing with me for 5 years transferred her account to another broker because her returns "weren't high enough." Over the 5 years she'd been with me, she had earned average annual returns in the high 20s. In 1999 alone, her mutual funds were up 58 percent, 32 percent, and 12 percent, respectively. But a broker she met at a wedding convinced her he could quadruple her money within a year, so she decided to transfer her account to him. That was in March of 2000, the month that now marks (in hindsight, of course) the beginning of the tech-stock crumble. I haven't talked to her since, but I'll bet she wishes she were back in her boring old mutual funds.

Another client, husband and wife, conveniently forgot our entire risk–reward discussion that took place when we first started investing their small-business retirement plan assets in 1994. When they complained to me in 1999 of their 29.5 percent return, I pulled out their original investment policy guidelines, which called for anticipated returns of 8 percent to 10 percent— established at that level because they said they didn't want to assume too much risk. In the ensuing years, when their actual returns averaged 14 percent, they were very pleased. But in 1999, when the Nasdaq was up 86 percent, their 29.5 percent return suddenly seemed like peanuts. I pointed out that the vast majority of the Nasdaq's stellar gains that year were due to only a handful of stocks and that half of all Nasdaq stocks were actually down for the year. They admitted they hadn't heard that side of the story.

One of the saddest stories was told by the owner of a clothing store where my husband and I do business. One day in April 2000, this normally upbeat guy was uncharacteristically irritable and cantankerous. When we asked if everything was okay, he confided that he had taken out a second mortgage on his house, borrowed money from his in-laws, taken a cash advance on his credit cards, and put it all into a margin account at a brokerage firm. He lost everything, more than $200,000. Now all his savings were gone and he had to pay back the margin loan, the credit card companies, the in-laws, and the mortgage. No one should have to suffer like this. But the markets can be ruthless if you're not careful, and anyone who takes such huge risks unfortunately has no one but themselves to blame.

FEAR OF MISSING THE BOAT

What causes normally rational people to do irrational things with their money? Why would an otherwise sensible client fall for a sucker pitch by a broker who promised to quadruple her money in a year? Why would my risk-averse clients, who know that high returns and high risks usually go hand in hand, suddenly want to abandon a well thought out strategy and consider subjecting their (and their employees') retirement money to high risk? Why would a successful businessman take huge risks with his personal funds, going so far into debt that it will take years to recover?

The answer lies in the fact that these are unusual times. Like the tulip mania of the 1600s and the California gold rush of the 1800s, the technology boom of the late 1990s was a chance for ordinary people to acquire extraordinary wealth. Everyone seemed to be cashing in. People were afraid of missing the boat. So they assumed a "land grab" mentality and almost went into an altered state of consciousness, forgetting—or rather, repudiating—all the conventional wisdom about diversification and risk management in a desperate attempt to claim the wealth they felt they deserved, before it went away. Never in my career have I had such a difficult time convincing people that the only sure road to riches is through working, saving, and sensible investing. With everyone around them getting rich, they simply didn't want to hear it. And in some ways I don't blame them. Other people were doing it, so why not them?

Now that the boom is over and the greed that once consumed Wall Street has been balanced with a healthy dose of fear,
it's back to reality. To all of you who didn't strike it rich in the
technology boom of the late 1990s—which is most people—I'm
sorry that you did indeed miss the boat. It's unlikely we will ever
see market conditions like that again, where companies that are
actually losing money carry market valuations higher than some
of our best blue-chip stocks. Those were crazy times, and personally I'm glad they didn't last. They were an aberration and a
distraction, and they kept people from doing what they need to
do to get rich the old-fashioned way, which is what this book is
all about.

WHY WE WANT TO BE RICH

There is a national obsession with being rich. It pervades our
culture, from the popularity of the TV show *Who Wants to Be a
Millionaire* to the fact that gambling is now legal in 47 states.
This obsession comes at a time when our standard of living has
never been higher, when modern conveniences like videocas-
sette recorders and microwave ovens are so affordable that nearly
everyone has at least one. When I was growing up, these things
didn't even exist. Today we take them for granted and still they're
not enough. We want more. We want to be rich. And we want it
now. Why?

One reason is that the media has exposed us to much
greater wealth than we would otherwise be aware of if our world
were limited to our own neighborhoods and social circles. We
read about, and see pictures of, Bill Gates's 45,000-square-foot
mansion and Larry Ellison's private jet. And because they are
both self-made men (Ellison is the founder and chief executive of
Oracle Corp.), we believe it's within our power to have those
things too—or something close to it. By flipping the channels on
our TV, we can see beautiful people in designer gowns, exquis-
itely decorated homes in Aspen and Palm Beach, and relaxed

people enjoying lavish vacations in exotic parts of the world. We see all these trappings of wealth and we want them too.

Although none of us would care to admit it, keeping up with the Joneses is still prevalent in our culture. We want a bigger house, a newer car, a fancier vacation than the people on our block. But since flashy, conspicuous consumption is no longer chic, bragging rights these days often go to the one who takes the more rugged adventure vacation or has the most sturdy sport utility vehicle. What we're really after is social acceptance. As much as we all abhor the idea of keeping up with our neighbors this way, it's endemic in our culture, especially among upwardly mobile people who can't help showing off to their friends the evidence of their success. Once the cycle has been set in motion, it's very hard to break.

Some would say that our focus on wealth and materialism reflects a spiritual void that we are desperately trying to fill. It's not money we want, but love, community, and a sense of peace and well-being. But, not knowing how to get those things, we go after money instead, in the misguided belief that wealth will make us happy. Never mind that survey after survey shows that people value relationships and good health over money, or that many people think having a lot of money makes people greedy and insensitive. In today's fast-paced world it's hard to lead a truly spiritual life, so we fill the void with BMWs and designer handbags.

Or maybe we want to be rich because we just want not to have to worry about money. By amassing enough cash to last the rest of our lives, we could be free to work at something we really enjoy, to not work if we didn't want to, to pursue humanitarian activities like volunteerism or teaching, to live where we want to live, to send our kids to good colleges, and to be able to buy things without pinching every penny. We think that if we could just get a quick hit of about $10 million or $100 million, we could say goodbye to bills and bosses and create the life we really want. Furthermore, we think there's nothing unhealthy or unusual about this attitude. Indeed, we would be *less* materialistic and moneygrubbing if we had enough of a stash that we wouldn't have to worry about money ever again.

Why We Want It Now

It's not good enough to acquire wealth over time. We want it now. Let's face it. We're not used to waiting for things. Our society used to be a lot more patient than we are now, but microwave ovens, TV sound bites, and e-mail have trained us to expect instant gratification. Do you remember when TVs and radios had to "warm up" before they came on? Have you ever seen a replay of an old commercial? It seems to take forever to get its message across. Perhaps some law of physics explains why time seems to pass faster now, but the fact is that we want what we want when we want it. We don't want to wait.

So when we see game show contestants and lottery winners and dot-com executives walk away with millions, we think that's for us. Give it to us in one fell swoop with no work and no waiting. Same with stock market riches: Why sit in a mutual fund and earn mediocre returns year after year when we could simply pick the right stock and strike it rich overnight?

The rise of easy credit has also made us impatient when it comes to money. In the past, people had to save up for major purchases. Today, we use a credit card and start enjoying our purchases immediately. Then we want those pesky credit card balances to disappear as rapidly as they appeared. We're used to instant credit. Why not instant debt elimination?

What It's Costing Us

This drive to get rich—quickly—is taking a toll on our lives. The most extreme example of money-induced stress was the nationally reported story of Mark O. Barton, a day trader who walked into an Atlanta brokerage firm one day in July 1999 and opened fire on several people before turning the gun on himself. Clearly, he was a disturbed man, but were it not for the stresses of day trading, the incident might not have happened.

Gambling is on the rise, and problem gambling—where the compulsion to win causes psychological, financial, emotional, marital, legal, and other difficulties—is also up. The 1999 National Gambling Impact Study Commission estimates that of the 125 million Americans who gamble at least once a year, approximately 7.5 million have some form of gambling problem, with another 15 million at risk of developing a gambling problem. As problem gamblers move from the winning stage to the losing stage to the desperation stage, their view of money begins to change. It loses its traditional value as a means to buy needed things or provide financial security and becomes a necessary tool to keep the gambler in action. Like alcoholics and drug addicts, extreme problem gamblers lose jobs, families, their health, and sometimes their lives in their desperate attempt to win money.

Lotteries are fueling the get-rich-quick dream by offering the hope of instant wealth—never mind that a person has a better chance of being struck by lightning. The worst part is that state governments are targeting their messages to poor people who feel the lottery is their only way out. One survey of poor versus rich neighborhoods showed 140 lottery outlets in a poor neighborhood and just five in a wealthy neighborhood. Some people call lotteries a regressive tax—though voluntary, it's still a tax, paid by the people who can least afford it. If a lottery ticket buyer took that $2 per week and let it compound at 8 percent a year, she'd have more than $5,000 in 20 years. Five dollars a week would turn into nearly $13,000. In some people's minds, this is peanuts compared to the chance to win millions. Instead, they wind up with nothing and are out-of-pocket several thousand dollars they can ill afford.

The stock market holds great potential for building wealth, but not if it's misused in the attempt to get rich quick. Day trading, which involves buying a stock in the morning and selling it before the market closes—sometimes turning over the same stock several times in one day—makes brokerage firms rich but generally not the traders themselves. There are so many fees associated with the practice and it's so difficult to capture profits consistently, that most day traders lose money. Even ordinary people who aren't day traders pour huge sums into risky stocks and ignore the signs suggesting they're about to lose some or all of their investment. Someone very close to me put $100,000 into a stock when it was trading at $19 per share, convinced it was going to $100. It's now selling for less than $2 and he's still hanging on to it. By riding it all the way down, he violated two of Wall Street's basic rules: (1) Never fall in love with a stock and (2) cut your losses short. There are countless stories about people who have risked their retirement funds, their children's college funds, and even their homes on some high-flying stock they were sure would be their ticket to wealth. Some got out before losing it all. Others weren't so lucky. Those who lost their families and their self-respect in the process are the most tragic.

Pyramid schemes and other flaky "investment" deals have always been around. As long as people grasp at easy riches and haven't figured out that such schemes never work, there will be new suckers for these scams. A recent example involved a pyramid scheme called "Changing Lives" in Lewiston, Maine. It seemed innocent enough: People would ask their friends to join their group and pay $2,000 to the person who had been in the group the longest. When the senior members had collected $16,000, they left, allowing more recent additions to replace them in the top spot and reap the profits from the next group of recruits. When the attorney general shut it down and threatened prosecution unless people returned the money, the town went into a tizzy. Some of the money was returned to the original owners as directed. But not all of it, and the outstanding debts created rifts in friendships among people who had known each other for years. When money ruins relationships, the consequences are more far reaching than people imagine.

I won't say a lot about debt in this book because you know if you have it and if it's making you uncomfortable. You don't need me telling you to get out of debt because it's costing you a lot in interest charges, and so forth. But do keep in mind that high debt—or more accurately the stress caused by high debt—can make people do some pretty crazy things. Many of the people who buy lottery tickets or who have turned into problem gamblers or lost money in risky stock ventures were simply trying to find a way out of their high debt. "If I could just get a quick $20,000 or $50,000 or $100,000, I could pay all my bills and finally get my finances straightened out," they say. But the riches seldom come, the money spent on lottery tickets or bad stocks is down the drain, and the debt remains.

If you do have a debt problem, first work on removing any negative emotions attached to it. You're not a bad person. You're not stupid. You might have made some mistakes in the past (although they didn't seem like mistakes at the time), but what's done is done and wishing you'd done things differently won't help. Try to detach yourself emotionally from your personal balance sheet and approach it as if you were managing a business. If you think the liabilities are too high in relation to the assets, start accelerating debt repayment. But don't get all crazy about it. Just set some goals and work toward creating a healthy balance sheet. Understand that it won't happen overnight. It's always easier and faster to get into debt than to get out. If it makes you feel any better, you're not alone. In the 1990s, the total value of all outstanding household debt reached unprecedented highs in the United States, mounting to more than half a trillion dollars.

IS INSTANT WEALTH REALLY ALL IT'S CRACKED UP TO BE?

Did you know that sudden wealth can actually be bad for you? This relatively new phenomenon has been studied by financial advisors and psychotherapists alike as more and more people fall into huge sums of money and don't know how to handle it. We've all heard stories about lottery winners whose lives changed completely—often not for the better—after winning the jackpot. They say their relationships with friends became strained, either because the friends expected the lottery winners to give them money, or the friends became so envious that it tainted the relationship. The newly wealthy people weren't sure how to act around their friends: Should they pay for dinner or buy them lavish gifts now that they could afford it, or would doing so throw it up in the friends' faces that they now had all this money? No matter how hard the lottery winners tried to keep things normal, the mere fact that they had won the money—and that their friends had weird feelings about it—changed everything. In interviews, some lottery winners actually said they wished they could have their old lives back. Who wants to be rich and friendless?

People who inherit money have all kinds of mixed emotions about it. First, most people are uncomfortable reaping monetary benefit from a death. Then, depending on their relationship with the departed, they may feel guilt, anger, sadness, and a variety of other emotions that complicate their feelings about the money. You can't spend with abandon when in the back of your mind is the nagging thought that if your loved one were still around, you wouldn't have the money to spend. If you really miss the person who died, just looking at the bank balance or receiving the monthly brokerage statements can remind you of his or her absence and make you sad all over again. This is not to say people who inherit money are necessarily worse off for it, but it can be a lot more complicated than people think.

Another fact of instant wealth is that it can kill ambition. Oh, no, you say, pointing out that you'd still be a productive, functioning member of society no matter how much money you came into. Why, then, is the Getty family in such a mess? Why did Jessie O'Neill, who inherited $3 million at age 28, write a book called *The Golden Ghetto: The Psychology of Affluence* (Hazelden, 1996) and devote her life to helping heirs and heiresses deal with the psychological aspects of sudden wealth? I have several clients—we call them "trust fund babies"—who inherited way too much money at far too early an age. They don't need to work, so they spend their time on the golf course while their friends are out working hard and making something of their lives. Let's face it, most of us would think long and hard about working if we suddenly didn't have to anymore. It can be very easy to slip into a life of indolence when there's no motivation to work. And without a productive outlet for a person's talents and skills, self-esteem suffers, the downward spiral begins, and the idle wealthy soon discover that they can't find meaningful work, even if they wanted to. This situation doesn't have to happen, but it's one more complication that can arise when a person comes into a lot of money all at once.

Then there's the sheer responsibility of handling all that wealth. If you think you worry too much about money now, just wait until you have a lot of it. Then you have to worry about managing it and keeping it away from the tax man, not to mention all those crazy people who like to sue rich people at the drop of a hat just because they have money. When you don't have much money, you don't have a lot of decisions to make. When you have a lot of it, you're faced with many decisions about what to do with it. How much can you spend now and on what? How much should you save for the future? How should you invest it? What about tax planning? Estate planning? Philanthropy? If you think your life is complicated, talk to someone who spends his or her day talking to stockbrokers, accountants, and lawyers, and at the end of the day still has to make the ultimate decisions about what to do with the money. It makes you want to opt for a life of voluntary simplicity. Has it ever occurred to you that you're not as rich as you'd like to be because subconsciously you're not ready for the responsibility of managing such a large amount of money? Just a thought. Read the rest of this book and you'll be prepared to handle anything.

LET'S GET REAL

Enough talk about people who got poor trying to get rich or people whose lives were ruined by sudden wealth. There's nothing wrong with money or the honest pursuit of it. Obviously I believe that, or I wouldn't have written this book and I wouldn't be in the profession I'm in. And obviously you don't see anything wrong in attempting to increase your net worth or you wouldn't have bought this book.

However, if you're expecting a sure, quick, painless road to riches, you're reading the wrong book. I wrote this book because of all the craziness today surrounding the pursuit of wealth. People want it fast. They want it easy. They want it without risk. And they want too much of it for their own good. They've lost sight of the basic principles surrounding wealth creation because there've been too many exceptions hyped up in the media. Most people acquire wealth by working hard and investing wisely. Sure, it's possible to get lucky and have a pot of money dumped in your lap that you didn't have to work for. *But that's the exception*. If you keep hoping that will happen, you won't do what you must to obtain the wealth that's waiting for you. You have to exchange your dreams for concrete planning and replace passive waiting with focused action.

THE SEVEN PRINCIPLES OF WEALTH CREATION

Let's quickly review the basic principles of wealth building. These are very elementary and intuitively you know they're all true. But in the frenzy to cash in on the dot-com revolution, whether you were an active participant or had your nose pressed up against the glass, you may have lost sight of them. Even if you've heard them before, they'll have more meaning now, especially if you are one of the casualties of the now-deflated Internet stock bubble.

1. The surest way to get money is to work for it.

When you're starting at zero, without a stockpile of cash to put to work for you, your most reliable source of income is yourself. Think about it. You can make millions of dollars over your lifetime, simply by exchanging your time and labor for cash. People who think of themselves as wage slaves underestimate their own cash-generating value and also fail to appreciate a society that allows them to make their own way in the world. If you don't like your job, you can get another one. If you want to make more money, you can ask for a raise or train for a promotion or new career. You can even start your own business or become self-employed and essentially name your own price. We tend to take our free-market system for granted, but many immigrants to the United States are amazed at how easy it is to make money here simply by applying yourself and working hard, an opportunity not possible in many other countries. You say you want to be rich? It's easy. Go to work! As you'll see in Chapter 2, that's how most people do it today, even if their labors are sometimes aided by ingenuity and a little luck.

2. The surest way to have money is to save it.

Money is like energy. It never disappears, it just gets exchanged into something else. Unfortunately, daily living forces us to exchange most of our money into things like food, shelter, clothing, and the occasional vacation. If we didn't have these needs, we could hang on to more of it and eventually become rich. Most people who aren't as rich as they'd like to be automatically associate money with spending. The first thing they think about when they contemplate winning the lottery or otherwise coming into a big sum of money is what they would spend it on. (Come on, admit it. You've done it too.) Do you know how rich people approach money? They think about preserving it, sheltering it from taxes, using it to make more money, and eventually passing it down to the next generation. Nonrich people enjoy money for what it can buy, which means they never keep it around very long. Rich people enjoy money for its own sake, which means they accumulate it and derive pleasure from the sheer fact of having it and making it grow. You don't have to be mercenary or have an unhealthy relationship with money to become rich. But shifting your focus from spending to saving would make it easier to hold on to more of your money. With this approach, you let it work for you instead of the other way around.

3. The surest way to build wealth is to let it compound.

Compound interest has been called the eighth wonder of the world. It truly is amazing how money grows when it builds earnings on top of earnings. Here's an example of how it works. If you were to invest $10,000 at a compounded rate of 10 percent, it would take 47 years to earn your first million. But it would take only 7 years to earn your second million, because the bigger your investment grows, the more earnings it generates. And those earnings generate earnings on their own in a kind of snowball effect. The rich keep getting richer because the money rolls in faster than they can spend it. But there's one key to compounding: You have to start with something. Seed money, even a small amount, is absolutely essential to get the compounding going. If you can add to it regularly, so much the better. But don't think that just because you don't have much money to start with that it's not worth the bother. Even $50 a month—the price of dinner for two—will be worth nearly $30,000 in 20 years if compounded at 8 percent. Increase your savings by 10 percent every year and you'll have more than $72,000.

4. Sometimes it's wise to take risks.

The only way to earn high investment returns is to take some risks. This is one of the basic tenets of investing. Depending on the type of investment and how much time you're willing to give it, the consequences of taking these risks may be one or more of the following: You could lose all of your money. You could lose some of your money. You could watch the value of your investment go up and down but not really lose any money because you don't need to sell it yet; in other words, the investment has good long-term potential and you're willing to hold it in exchange for the opportunity to earn high returns down the road. Paradoxically, the rich, who can afford to take risks because they have so much money to spare, don't really need to. They can keep getting richer by letting their money compound at even a low rate of return. The nonrich who are trying to become rich must take some risks in order to get where they want to be. But intelligent risk taking is the key. More about this Chapter 7.

5. Sometimes it's better to avoid risk.

Some risks are worth taking, others are not. One way to determine whether a risk is worth taking is to evaluate how devastating the consequences would be if the dreaded event were to occur. What if your house burned to the ground? What if you had a bad car accident? What if you were diagnosed with cancer? Because these events have the potential to cause financial ruin, it makes sense to transfer these types of risks to an insurance company. When evaluating any risk–reward proposition, the two-pronged question is always "what do I have to lose?" and "what will it cost me to avoid or minimize this risk?" Rich people obviously have more to lose, so they spend more on various kinds of insurance, including umbrella policies, which protect their fortunes from miscellaneous unforeseen disasters. Nonrich people don't need to spend as much on insurance because they don't have as much to lose. Once the basic risks are covered, they are better off directing any discretionary income to their savings and investment accounts.

6. The surest way to save taxes is by contributing to a retirement plan.

Every dollar not paid out in taxes can be used to generate more wealth. Rich people understand this, which is why they hire smart accountants and lawyers to help them find various legal ways to save on taxes. But the surest and easiest way to save taxes is available to anyone who works for a living: Simply contribute part of your salary to a retirement plan. Here's how it works. Let's say you earn $50,000 a year. If you report the full $50,000 in income and have average deductions, you'll pay about $8,551 in taxes. But if you contribute $5,000 to a retirement plan, you'll pay just $7,151 in taxes, a savings of $1,400. So not only do you have $5,000 safely tucked away in a retirement plan that's growing tax-deferred for your benefit later on, you also have $1,400 that you otherwise wouldn't have. You can invest this money in a regular after-tax account and get it started growing as well. Keep in mind that with this strategy you are no worse off than if you didn't make the retirement plan contribution. You are not sacrificing the $5,000, because it's still your money—you just can't get to it yet. Anyone who wants to be rich must think long term and be prepared to postpone the present use of money in order to build it into something greater in the future.

7. To generate wealth, give some away.

I'm not going to suggest that you send money to charitable organizations if you're not yet in a financial position to do so. In fact, it may be better for you to be a little stingy with your hard-earned money until you can establish a solid savings plan that's growing and compounding. I am talking about a broader definition of wealth and approaching life with a spirit of generosity. Sometimes people can be so focused on money as the only measure of wealth that they fail to see it in a larger context. They are so intent on saving a few bucks here and there that it completely consumes them. This is not the way to get rich. A better way is to share your wealth as you go through life, and by wealth I mean whatever you have in abundance, which at this stage of your life may be time and talent if not money. All the major religions teach this tenet, and I've seen in my own life that the more you give away, the more comes back to you. The principle works in mysterious ways, but it does work.

CHAPTER TWO

FAMOUS BILLIONAIRES

How They Did It

Money is the seed of money, and the first guinea is sometimes more difficult to acquire than the second million.

Jean Jacques Rousseau

My formula for success. Rise early, work late, strike oil.

J. Paul Getty

WHEN WE LOOK AT RICH PEOPLE and covet what they have, we're looking at a snapshot in time. In most cases, we're seeing the culmination of many years of planning, working, and building to get where they are. We see the glorious mansion and splendid gardens, not the blueprints and messy construction that preceded the completion of this perfect monument to the rewards that await those who toil. We all know of people who have had great wealth dropped into their laps. But what is there to learn from them? That we were born into the wrong family? That we're not as lucky as they are? How does that help us in our pursuit of wealth? If we're going to spend our time envying rich people, we should do it constructively—by looking at how they got rich and drawing parallels, or lessons, that we can apply to our own lives. In this chapter we look at some famous billionaires past and present in order to examine how they did it.

HE WENT FROM ZERO TO BEING
THE RICHEST MAN IN AMERICA

In the late 19th century John D. Rockefeller built the biggest fortune this country had ever known. And he built it from the ground up. Unlike fellow industrialists Vanderbilt, Astor, and Morgan, who also built huge fortunes around the same time, Rockefeller did not have the benefit of generational wealth. He was born on a small farm in upstate New York on July 8, 1839, the second of six children. The family lived in modest circumstances, but Rockefeller showed an interest in making money from an early age. His first business venture was raising a flock of turkeys on the farm. At the age of 10 he lent a neighboring farmer $50 at 7 percent interest and later said, "from that time on I was determined to make money work for me."

His first job was as a bookkeeper for a dry goods merchant; he earned $4 per week and developed a real understanding of how money works. He kept a personal ledger in which he meticulously recorded his income, expenses, investments, and charity. His only interest outside of business was the Baptist church, to which he gave 10 percent of his income. When his employers refused to increase his salary, he realized that his future was limited unless he went out on his own. He managed to save $1,000, borrowed another $1,000 from his father (at 10 percent interest), and formed a partnership with a friend, Maurice B. Clark. Initially, the business sold dry goods. But once the nation's first oil well was drilled at Titusville in western Pennsylvania in 1859, Rockefeller and Clark saw a new opportunity. Along with several other partners they invested $4,000 to build their first oil refinery in Cleveland, Ohio.

After a few years of successful pumping, Rockefeller and his partners disagreed on how the business should be managed. Rockefeller wanted to reinvest the profits to continually improve and expand the business; the others disagreed. So Rockefeller bought them out for the then-exorbitant sum of $72,500. He later described this event as "one of the most important in my life. It was the day that determined my career." In the ensuing years, demand for oil grew as people began to illuminate their homes with kerosene lamps and factories used it for lubrication. In 1870, Rockefeller formed Standard Oil of Ohio and soon was refining 29,000 barrels of crude oil a day.

Rockefeller went on to acquire 23 oil companies in his race for total control of the oil industry and even gained control of pipelines so he would not be dependent on the railroads for transportation. In 1882, he merged all of his companies into the Standard Oil Trust, which dominated 80 percent of America's oil refining business and 90 percent of America's pipelines. In 1911, the U.S. Supreme Court found the Standard Oil Trust in violation of the Sherman Antitrust Act of 1890, and ordered the company be dissolved into its 39 subsidiary companies. By this time Rockefeller's fortune, which had been expanded by investments in railroads, banks, and real estate, was worth $1 billion.

A few points about Rockefeller's story are worth noting. First and most obvious is that he discovered very early in life, through direct experience, that money can be used to make more money. By lending the neighboring farmer $50 at 7 percent interest, he saw how money could be increased just by deploying it properly. Second, he discovered early in his working career the limitations of being paid a salary. As long as someone else was deciding how much to pay him, there was nothing he could do to significantly increase that amount. Rockefeller wasn't opposed to working, but the type of work he preferred was finding ways to make his money grow.

Also, Rockefeller was a successful businessman even before oil was discovered in 1859. He and Clark could have continued their dry goods business, growing and expanding it to generate a small fortune without ever taking on the risk of a new venture. And it's important to view the situation from the perspective of 1860 America. Today, we know how vital oil is to everyday life: It runs our cars and lights and heats our homes. But back then, no one had thought much about this sticky black substance or how it could be used in American life. How could Rockefeller have foreseen the demand for something that in all of human history people had been able to get along just fine without? What was he thinking when he turned away from a thriving business to embrace a brand-new industry whose potential had not even begun to be contemplated? We could put this question to anyone who charts new territory in the business world. They must be able to envision something that the rest of us cannot.

OPPORTUNITIES WERE EVERYWHERE

Twentieth-century America is teeming with examples of burgeoning new industries that bestowed fame and fortune on people who weren't necessarily smarter or richer than anyone else but who possessed a certain canniness when it came to envisioning something no one else could see. These extraordinary people took what would seem to us to be enormous risks but to them were just necessary steps to get from here to there—or should I say there to here? Thanks to the early industrialists, America now has the highest standard of living in the world. Who among us doesn't take for granted the fact that we can buy fresh produce just hours after it has been harvested and enjoy light and heat at the flip of a switch?

The building of the transcontinental railroad in the 19th century opened up business opportunities that had not existed before. Prior to the building of the railroad, most goods consumed by Americans were produced locally. Small factories turned out dry goods and sold them to commission agents (like Rockefeller and Clark) who traveled from one dry goods store to another. Most people were farmers who raised food for their own families, perhaps selling to a few neighbors as well.

Once railroads were built, farmers could sell to many markets, not just those close to home. And whole new industries, such as refrigeration and meatpacking, opened up so farmers and butchers could take advantage of the railroads to transport their products. Today we think of the Internet as this amazing phenomenon that has the potential to change life as we know it and produce fortunes for those smart enough to get in early. We look at the so-called Internet bubble that blew up and immediately deflated at the turn of the 21st century and figure we must have missed it. If we didn't get in and get out of stocks of Internet companies when they jumped 5-fold, 10-fold, 100-fold, we kick ourselves for having missed the opportunity of a lifetime.

But placed in historical perspective, the building of the Internet is akin to the building of the railroad or, after the invention of the automobile, the transcontinental highways. The big money wasn't made on the actual construction. It wasn't even made on the picks and shovels used in construction. It was made on the many opportunities that arose after these thoroughfares were built—opportunities that were unimaginable when the railroads and highways first went in because the full impact of easy, fast, widespread transportation hadn't yet become clear. It took years of contemplation and ideas building on top of each other for the real money-making opportunities to present themselves.

For example, Adolphus Busch, head of the Anheuser-Busch Company, was one of the first brewers to understand how the railroad could increase beer sales. Instead of being limited to local markets or relying on riverboats to carry kegs to distant cities, he saw the potential for railroads to carry beer from coast to coast. But the spark of the idea was just the beginning. He then had to consider shipping costs, the establishment of depots, and how to keep the beer cold en route. Here his idea converged with someone else's. A butcher named Gustavus Swift had been experimenting with refrigeration so he could sell meat to distant markets. After several failed attempts, he and engineer Andrew Chase developed the first workable insulated railroad car, which had ice compartments under the car's roof. To replace the melting ice, Swift also arranged for ice depots along the railroad's route, giving Busch the way to keep his beer cold in transit. Just as New Yorkers could enjoy beef produced in Chicago, Texans could drink beer made in Missouri. And then refrigerated freight cars made it possible for California fruit and produce to be sent to the East Coast. It took many people working on solutions to different problems to establish conditions for any one person to strike it rich.

That's how it will be in the 21st century, too. We can't yet predict which industries and businesses hold the greatest money-making potential because too many things have to happen first. But we can train ourselves to be on the lookout for exciting opportunities. We can't emulate exactly the work of John D. Rockefeller or Adolphus Busch or anyone else who seized opportunity and struck it rich, because the opportunities will be different next time. And most likely they will be seen only by those who dare to look at the world in a different way—like Rockefeller's ability to foresee demand for a commodity whose primary applications hadn't even been invented yet, or Busch's refusal to let a little detail like lack of refrigeration stand in the way of getting his beer to market.

HE SAW A NEED AND FOUND A WAY TO FILL IT

By the 1920s, the giant industrialists had established strong footholds in industries such as steel and oil refining. Not only did these industries depend on economies of scale to reach their full potential, but small businesses were virtually excluded from participation due to the monopolistic practices of industrialists such as Rockefeller and Andrew Carnegie. (It should be noted that both Rockefeller and Carnegie became two of the world's greatest philanthropists, sharing their extraordinary wealth with society, presumably to make up for ruthless business practices while they were building their fortunes.)

In other words, early 20th century America was not a good time for small business. That fact didn't keep people from trying, however. America was founded on the notion of rugged individualism, and entrepreneurship certainly fits with the American character. But more than half of all startups failed within the first four years, primarily due to inadequate financing. Thanks to J. P. Morgan's strides in investment banking, plenty of money was available for big businesses, but there weren't many ways for small business owners to obtain the capital they needed to grow. Most new businesses were started with personal savings and loans from friends and family members. Entrepreneurs were unable to get loans from banks unless they had suitable liquid assets which the bank could seize if need be—not unlike going to a pawn shop.

Amadeo Peter Giannini[*] (who was not technically a billionaire for reasons you'll discover in a moment) recognized the need small businesses had for capital and sought to democratize the banking business. Although not born to humble circumstances like Rockefeller, Giannini had the benefit of an immigrant's perspective. In some immigrant groups it was common for members to pool funds and make loans to those wanting to enter business, a practice that continues to this day. In reflecting

[*]"America's Banker: A. P. Giannini," D. Kadlec, www.time.com/time/time100/builder/profile/giannini.html.

on the banking business, which in the 1920s catered primarily to wealthy people, Giannini thought that small depositors and borrowers had something to offer one another. His idea was to welcome small depositors and pool their deposits to make loans to small businessmen.

He encountered opposition at every turn. The money center banks in New York and Chicago served only corporations and the very wealthy. The larger banks in California, where Giannini lived, also made loans only to the most creditworthy customers. Even Columbus Savings and Loan, a local bank in the Italian section of San Francisco on whose board he sat, refused to consider small merchants hoping to start or expand a business. Finally, in 1909 he took $20,000 of his own money and raised $130,000 from friends and relatives and formed his own savings institution called the Bank of Italy in a converted saloon across the street from Columbus Savings and Loan. He kept the bartender on as a teller.

Giannini's goal was to open banking to the masses. He advertised for depositors and publicized his lending services to local businesses, a practice unheard of in the white shoe banking business. He even made what were called "character loans" to people he knew to be honest and hardworking. Eighteen months after it opened, the Bank of Italy's loans exceeded its deposits by more than $200,000. When the 1906 San Francisco earthquake hit, Giannini dashed out of bed, quickly hitched a team of horses to a wagon and went to the bank, where he sifted through the rubble and salvaged more than $2 million in gold, coins, and securities. While other banks were closed for earthquake repairs, Giannini erected a tent on a pier, set up a desk with a plank and two barrels, and made loans "on a face and a signature" to people who needed money to rebuild their lives. Two days after the earthquake, he advertised in the *San Francisco Chronicle*: "Bank of Italy Now Opened for Regular Business." This ad launched the rebuilding of San Francisco, established Giannini's legacy, and set in motion an expansion plan that ultimately led to the formation of the second largest bank in the United States today, the Bank of America.

By the time of Giannini's death in 1949, other banks had followed his example of seeking deposits from ordinary Americans and making loans to small businesses. Giannini had democratized banking, pioneered home mortgages and auto loans, and made capital accessible to everyone. At the time of his death, Giannini's estate was worth less than $500,000. This was by choice. He could have been a billionaire but disdained great wealth, believing it would make him lose touch with the people he wanted to serve. For years he accepted virtually no pay, and upon being granted a surprise $1.5 million bonus one year promptly gave it all to the University of California. "Money itch is a bad thing," he once said. "I never had that trouble." When asked about the reasons for his success he said, "I have worked without thinking of myself. This is the largest factor in whatever success I have attained."

What parallels can we draw from Giannini's story that might apply to an unknowable future? Obviously, we can't open up banking to the little guy; that's already been done. But perhaps we can glean some insights from the way he identified opportunity and ran his business that might carry over into a new era. First was Giannini's unique perspective on an industry that had always operated in a set manner, serving a set clientele, and excluding a set group of people—Giannini among them. As a second generation American, and a Californian, he had the benefit of not being entrenched in a system that everyone else took for granted. Indeed, some of our country's greatest pioneers have taken the statement "but we've always done it this way" and eagerly turned it into a challenge. Not without tremendous opposition, of course.

And that's the second lesson we can gain from this story. In early 20th century America, the financiers ruled everything. They controlled who could (and could not) have access to capital, which pretty much determined who would have the power and financial success. The financiers were even cozy with the legislators, influencing the passage of laws such as those designed to keep Giannini from expanding his banking network in the 1920s.

But Giannini pressed on, convinced he was doing the right thing and refusing to let the opposition destroy his dream.

The third lesson is the ultimate paradox. Giannini was not interested in making money for himself. He was on a mission to democratize banking for the little guy, and he feared that if he were to become rich himself, he would lose his affinity with the person he was trying to help. This idea seems to fit with my observation of successful entrepreneurs. I'll bet if you were to ask 100 rich businesspeople to name the number one factor that drove their success, few, if any, would say "the money."

HE CHANGED THE WAY WE SHOP AND MADE BILLIONS FOR HIS FAMILY

Sam Walton is the perfect example of a billionaire who didn't live like one. He drove an old truck and had a plain, down-home style that reflected his Arkansas roots. He eschewed the limelight and quietly went about building his empire until Forbes discovered in 1985 that his holdings in Wal-Mart stock made him the richest man in America. Actually, the Walton Family Trust owned what was then about $20 billion worth of stock. Although Sam Walton lived very simply, he was unusually canny about money. On the advice of his wealthy father-in-law, who told him that the best way to avoid estate taxes was to give away assets before they appreciated, he set up a family trust to save estate and gift taxes long before his fortune was established.

Despite his father-in-law's wealth, Sam Walton was a self-made man. He worked before and after school from a very young age, milking the family cows every morning, delivering the bottled milk after school, and delivering newspapers and selling magazine subscriptions on the side. After graduating from the University of Missouri in 1940, he started work as a management trainee for J. C. Penney for $75 a week plus commissions. There Walton learned the basics of retailing and developed some of his management ideas such as calling workers "associates" and letting managers buy stakes in their stores to give them more of an investment in their stores' success. So when he had an opportunity to open his own small store—a Ben Franklin franchise in Newport, Arkansas—he knew what to do. He borrowed $20,000 from his father-in-law and scraped together $5,000 of his own savings and at the age of 27 took over his first store on September 1, 1945. The business did so well he was able to pay back his father-in-law after $2\frac{1}{2}$ years. He then went on to buy several more stores.

Sam Walton was always interested in saving money, and he figured other people were too. His approach to retailing was to get great deals from his suppliers, pass the savings on to his customers, and make up for the reduced margins with higher volume. Discounting was just starting to catch on in the early 1960s with the opening of Kmart and Target, but the Ben Franklin stores were slow to embrace the concept. Walton saw the writing on the wall and became convinced that if he didn't go into discounting, his variety store chain would be doomed. But to do it right, he needed money, more money than he could easily get his hands on. He made his pitch to the Ben Franklin executives and asked them to partner with him, but they turned him down, as did a few other retailing executives. As crazy as this seems in hindsight, it must be remembered that at the time, discounting was associated with dirty, dingy stores and shoddy merchandise. Sam Walton may have been able to visualize bright, clean stores where merchandise was sold at low prices, but no one else could. He ended up borrowing $350,000 from the bank using his wife's inheritance as collateral.

On July 2, 1962, he opened Wal-Mart Discount City in Rogers, Arkansas, promising "everyday low prices" and "satisfaction guaranteed." The significance of this event would take years to permeate through the American business landscape. Sam Walton, in his quest to lower the cost of living for all Americans, created a new way to sell merchandise and caused a sea change in the world of retailing. At the same time he was giving rural shoppers quality merchandise at low prices, he was forcing thousands of mom-and-pop store owners to find a new way to make a living.

Sam Walton is both revered and reviled for the impact his Wal-Mart stores have had on the retail industry. People hate that he's littered the landscape with ugly box stores and inspiring others like Circuit City and Home Depot to do likewise. They hate that he's exploited suppliers and squeezed margins so tight that a lot of manufacturing has been moved overseas where workers, including children, are worked hard and paid little. But they love the fact that they can buy inexpensive clothes and luxuries such as stereos and microwave ovens that they might not have been able to afford had Sam Walton not entered the scene.

Regardless of how you feel about Sam Walton and his impact on American life, his story contains some valuable lessons. First, Walton wasn't afraid of debt. There were periods when he was tremendously overextended, often with his personal assets on the line. But he knew he had to leverage himself to the hilt in order to realize his dream of "reducing the cost of living for all Americans." Most people would not feel comfortable with the amount of debt Walton took on, especially with so little assurance that any particular venture would produce enough cash to service the debt. But then, most people aren't billionaires.

Second, Walton craved information and insight. Not one to think he had all the answers, he was like a sponge whenever he was around anyone who had anything to do with retail. He traveled around the country visiting store after store, noting how merchandise was displayed and priced, and talking to store managers about how they managed inventory. He asked question after question and took notes on his ubiquitous yellow legal pad. He even attended an IBM school in upstate New York as early as 1966 to find out if he might have any use for a computer. While he was there, he hired the smartest guy in the class to come to Bentonville, Arkansas, and computerize his operations.

Sam Walton is best known for his relentless drive to squeeze every penny out of the merchandising system wherever it lay—in the stores, in the manufacturers' profit margins or with the middleman—all in the service of driving prices lower than anyone could imagine. He knew early on that careful attention to inventory management and logistics was key to keeping margins low and volume high. Although he hated to spend money, he managed to part with the funds needed to invest in technology. Wal-Mart became the icon of just-in-time inventory control and sophisticated logistics—the ultimate user of information as a competitive advantage. Funny how this down-home guy from the rural south, who would pick up investment bankers from the airport in his dirty, beaten up truck, ended up becoming one of the first chief executive officers (CEOs) of the information age.

If we're going to study rich people, we might as well look at them warts and all. And Sam Walton certainly had a few. The private Sam Walton was known to be a workaholic, who started his day as early as 4:00 A.M. and kept going well into the night. He traveled a lot, spent little time with his wife and four children when he was home, and even planned family vacations around store visits. It's been surmised that this pattern was set early in life, when Walton absorbed himself in work of one kind or another to avoid being around his quarreling parents. Although several books have been written about Sam Walton, little is known about his private life because he simply refused to talk about it. Sam Walton may have had a deeper understanding of retailing than anyone on Earth, but his life was hardly balanced. Lack of balance is often one of the hazards of becoming a billionaire.

HE'S BEEN CALLED THE WORLD'S GREATEST INVESTOR

Even the very likable Warren Buffett has been accused of neglecting his family in his focused pursuit of wealth. Buffett made his money investing in other people's businesses, so if hands-on management à la Sam Walton is not your style, you may lean toward Buffett's approach. Warren Buffett was #4 on the Forbes 2000 list of the richest people in America, with an estimated net worth of $28 billion. [Sam Walton's widow and four children collectively occupied spot #7, with $17 billion each; put them altogether and they'd be #1 with $85 billion, beating out Bill Gates who stood at #1 with $63 billion. Larry Ellison was #2 with $58 billion and Paul Allen #3 with $36 billion. Some of these numbers have changed as stock prices have risen and (mostly) fallen.]

Warren Buffett is the chairman of a company called Berkshire Hathaway, a textile company that was incorporated in 1889. But when you think of Berkshire Hathaway, don't think of textile mills and manufacturing operations. Those have long been closed. Under Buffett's direction, the company now owns interests in a variety of different businesses, ranging from insurance to candy. The nature of these businesses, and how Buffett happens to choose them, is the subject of intense study by investors small and large. Buffett has quite simply been called the world's greatest investor. And with good reason. According to Berkshire's 2000 annual report, the company has achieved annual compound investment returns of 23 percent over the past 36 years.

If you've been a student of the stock market for any length of time, you know what an extraordinary record this is. But in his usual humble style, Buffett has lately downplayed expectations for the future, saying that in the past he was able to buy stocks and businesses at far more attractive prices than he can today. Also, he's somewhat limited by Berkshire's "large capital base" (i.e., too much money), which restricts the kinds of investments he can make. Fortunately (or unfortunately) you and I don't have that problem. Buffett has the advantage of being able to buy whole companies, but you and I can follow his same criteria to buy 100 shares in any public corporation. That's the great thing about the stock market.

Warren Buffett got started in the stock market in a very natural way: his father was a stockbroker. At age 8, he began reading his father's books on the stock market, and when he was 11, he recorded stock prices on a chalkboard at Harris Upham in Omaha, Nebraska, where his father worked. That same year, 1941, he bought his first shares of stock, Cities Service Preferred. During his teens the family lived in Washington, D.C., where Buffett's father served as a congressman. Buffett earned money by working two paper routes. With his savings he bought reconditioned pinball machines for $25 each which he placed in local barbershops. Soon he was taking home $50 a week. With a high

school friend he bought a 1934 Rolls Royce for $350 and rented
it out for $35 a day. By the time he graduated from high school
at 16, Buffett had saved $6,000.

During his senior year at the University of Nebraska, Buffett
read Benjamin Graham and David Dodd's classic book, *Security
Analysis*. This book so influenced Buffett that after receiving his
college degree he went to New York to study with Ben Graham at
the Columbia Graduate Business School. Graham, who had lost
everything in the stock market crash of 1929, preached the importance of understanding a company's intrinsic value and said
that without some idea of a company's true worth, the "tides of
pessimism and euphoria which sweep the market" could mislead
investors into overvaluing or undervaluing a stock. This mathe-
matical approach appealed to Buffett's sense of numbers, and
after receiving his master's degree he went to work in Graham's
investment firm in New York, where he became fully immersed in
his mentor's investment philosophy.

In 1956, Graham's firm disbanded and Buffett returned to
Omaha. At the age of 25, he put together a limited partnership
with seven limited partners who together contributed $105,000.
Buffett, the general partner, started with $100. The deal was that
the limited partners would receive 6 percent annually on their
money, plus 75 percent of the profits above this bogey. Buffett
would get the remaining 25 percent. He promised the partners
that "our investments will be chosen on the basis of value, not
popularity" and over the next 13 years, he compounded the
money at an annual rate of 29.5 percent. Although the Dow
Jones Industrial Average declined in five of those years, Buffett's
partnership never had a down year. It was during these years—
1962 to be exact—that Buffett began buying the ailing Berkshire
Hathaway.

In 1969, Buffett disbanded the partnership saying he found
the market highly speculative. The "nifty fifty" stocks, including
Avon, IBM, Polaroid, and Xerox, were dominating the market
and their prices had risen, in Buffett's opinion, sky high. He said
in the annual report, "I will not abandon a previous approach
whose logic I understand, although I find it difficult to apply,

even though it may mean foregoing large and apparently easy profits to embrace an approach which I don't fully understand, have not practiced successfully, and which possibly could lead to substantial permanent loss of capital." Buffett took his share of the partnership proceeds—$25 million—and gained control of Berkshire Hathaway.

In the late 1960s, while Berkshire's textile operations were limping along, the company purchased the outstanding stock of two insurance companies headquartered in Omaha: National Indemnity Company and National Fire & Marine Insurance Company. This marked the beginning of Berkshire's phenomenal success story. Today, Berkshire owns an insurance company, a newspaper publishing company, two aviation service companies, a furniture store, a candy company, a shoe company, and more. What about technology, you ask? Nope. Berkshire hasn't invested a penny in technology. Buffett says he doesn't understand it and he refuses to invest in anything he doesn't understand. This is despite his friendship with fellow billionaire Bill Gates and the fact that the two play bridge together whenever they can. When tech stocks were flying high in 1999, some observers dared to suggest that Buffett's approach was passé, that it was out of touch with the times, that his and Graham's belief in intrinsic value was as outdated as those quaint pinball machines Buffett once placed in barber shops. Although Buffett's investment performance has trailed the market averages of late, his value-based approach has been vindicated by the tech stock sell-off and the realization among investors that earnings really do matter.

If you're interested in knowing more about Buffett's investment strategy—specifically the calculations he uses to determine intrinsic value—read *Buffett: The Making of an American Capitalist* by Roger Lowenstein (Doubleday, 1996) and *The Warren Buffett Way* by Roger G. Hagstrom (Wiley, 1997). You can also access Berkshire's annual reports in which Buffett expounds his investment philosophy at great length on the Web at www.berkshirehathaway.com.

In a nutshell, the "Warren Buffett Way" as described in Hagstrom's book (pp. 225–235) consists of four steps.

Step 1: Turn off the stock market. Remember that the stock market is manic-depressive. Of course, this behavior creates opportunities, particularly when shares of outstanding businesses are available at irrationally low prices. But just as you would not take direction from an advisor who exhibited manic-depressive tendencies, neither should you allow the market to dictate your actions. Buffett believes that if you plan on owning shares in an outstanding business for a number of years, what happens in the market on a day-to-day basis is inconsequential. He once said, "After we buy a stock, consequently, we would not be disturbed if markets closed for a year or two. We don't need a daily quote on our 100 percent position in See's or H. H. Brown to validate our well being. Why, then, should we need a quote on our 7 percent interest in Coke?" The only question on your mind should be, "has anybody done anything foolish lately that will allow me an opportunity to buy a good business at a great price?"

Step 2: Don't worry about the economy. First, no one can predict the economy, so it's foolish to try. Second, if you select stocks that will benefit by a particular economic environment, you inevitably invite turnover and speculation. Buffett prefers to buy businesses that have the opportunity to profit regardless of the economy.

Step 3: Buy a business, not a stock. Buffett's investment philosophy can be summed up in this paragraph from a recent annual report: "Whenever Charlie [Munger, his partner] and I buy common stocks . . . we approach the transaction as if we were buying into a private business. We look at the economic prospects of the business, the people in charge of running it, and the price we must pay. We do not have in mind any time or price for sale. Indeed, we are willing to hold a stock indefinitely so long as we expect the business to increase in intrinsic value at a satisfactory rate. When investing, we view ourselves as business analysts—not as market analysts, not as macro-economic analysts, and not even as security analysts." He only buys businesses he understands and that have a consistent operating history and favorable long-term prospects.

Step 4: Manage a portfolio of businesses. Unlike most investment professionals, Buffett does not believe in broad diversification. Because you are not following stock prices but rather investing in the best businesses available, you can do just fine owning ten or so carefully selected enterprises. He puts it this way: If the best business you own presents the least financial risk and has the most favorable long-term prospects, why would you put money into your twentieth favorite business rather than add money to the top choices? (I'll be covering the other side of this argument in Chapter 7.) Clearly, Buffett is an expert at investing and spends all of his time doing it. He acknowledges that not everyone has the time or inclination for such extensive due diligence. His advice to them: invest in an index fund and be done with it.

HE BUILT A DIFFERENT KIND OF COMPANY AND BECAME THE RICHEST MAN IN THE WORLD

Throughout most of 20th-century America we admired our billionaires from afar—not that there were that many of them. We'd check out Forbes's list of richest people, marvel that anyone could manage to amass *a billion dollars*, and assume that they lived in a world very different from ours. This rarified world of billionaires held a mystique that conjured up images of high finance and big business, hushed offices with mahogany paneling, and old, white, gray-haired men in elegant pin-striped suits who talked about Very Important Things. Then along came a guy named Bill Gates, who prefers to be called Bill (not William Gates III) and who, with his tousled hair and rumpled khakis, reminds us of the president of the math club in high school. The guy not only managed to amass a billion dollars, he became the richest man in the world! And we see this very ordinary-looking guy and think: *I could have done that!*

With his youth and middle-class upbringing, Bill Gates makes us think anybody could do what he did. You don't have to be born into the right lineage. You don't have to start out with lots of money. You don't even have to graduate from college! Just start a little company from scratch, grow it into a big company, and there you are: a billionaire. Two facts suggest that Bill's path to great wealth was not necessarily easy or accessible to everyone. First, Bill Gates is very, very smart (he got a perfect score on the math section of the scholastic aptitude test). Second, he worked very, very hard (he was probably the first computer geek to sleep under his desk during marathon programming sessions). Some would add a third element—that he's ruthless and competitive to a fault—but as we've seen, these features seem to be common among billionaires and may even be a requirement of the job.

Bill Gates was born in Seattle in 1956. His father is a successful attorney and his mother, who died a few years ago, served on the boards of several educational institutions, charities, and banks. Bill went to the prestigious Lakeside School, a private school that in the 1960s was fortunate enough to have a computer terminal hooked up to a mainframe. It was in Lakeside's computer room that Bill met Paul Allen, who was 2 years older than Bill. When Bill was 13, the two wrote their first program, a computerized tic-tac-toe game that could have been played faster with pencil and paper, but that gave them the thrill of being able to make a machine carry out their commands.

A few years later, Paul graduated and went to Washington State University in Spokane. Two years later Bill went to Harvard. By this time, Paul was bored by college and wanted to form a new company with Bill. He drove across the country and took a job as a programmer for Honeywell near Boston while he waited for Bill to graduate. Bill, meanwhile, was not exactly the model student at Harvard, skipping classes and engaging in all-night poker games. In January 1975, the two read in *Popular Electronics* about the "world's first microcomputer kit to rival commercial models," the Altair. They ordered the kit and spent five exhausting, almost sleepless weeks writing a BASIC program for it. They persuaded MITS, the small company in Albuquerque, New Mexico, that manufactured the Altair, to sell their program. When MITS offered them jobs, Allen quit his job at Honeywell and Bill took a leave from Harvard. In 1979, while still in Albuquerque and working for MITS, they formed their own company called Microsoft. The company sold computer programs, also known as software.

By 1980, Microsoft had moved to Seattle and had 35 employees. Recognizing the need for management help, Bill called his old friend at Harvard, Steve Ballmer, who had spent some time as a product development manager at Procter & Gamble and was currently enrolled in business school at Stanford. Ballmer was reluctant to quit business school, but after Gates offered him part ownership of the company, he agreed. Good thing. By 2000, Ballmer's net worth of $17 billion earned him a spot at #7 on Forbes' 2000 list of richest Americans. Ballmer is credited with having played a major part in the company's phenomenal growth, calling for new hirings when Bill wanted to save money, for example, and aggressively pursuing new growth opportunities throughout the 1990s.

A turning point for Microsoft came when Bill was introduced to an IBM executive by his mother, who knew him through her board involvement (proving that family connections do help). Bill was in negotiations to buy Q-DOS, a program that had been created by a small rival company called Seattle Computer, when it signed a deal with IBM to supply the operating system for every computer IBM produced. Microsoft ended up purchasing Q-DOS for $50,000, made a few engineering adjustments to turn it into MS-DOS, then turned around and offered it to IBM. But rather than charging IBM a flat fee for the program, Microsoft *licensed* it instead. This meant that Microsoft would make money on every computer that had the operating system installed on it. The decision to license MS-DOS was probably the single most important decision Microsoft ever made. It turned the company into a virtual cash machine, enabling it to earn fees on nearly every computer sold, and then charging those computer owners again and again when it upgraded the operating system every few years.

All this cash allowed Microsoft to create new products and dominate virtually every marketplace it decided to enter. Although most rich businesspeople will tell you it's not about the money, when you're running a public corporation and have to answer to shareholders, it very definitely *is* about the money. And Microsoft has been very good to its shareholders. Whatever you may think about Microsoft's ruthless business practices, the company cannot be faulted for fulfilling its obligations to shareholders, many of whom became millionaires while Gates was amassing his billions.

THE INTERNET WHIZ KIDS SHOW HOW QUICKLY WEALTH CAN COME . . . AND GO

In the mid-1990s ideas about companies and profits started to change. Suddenly it became fine for public companies not to have earnings as long as they had a good idea and some inkling of how they might make money in the future. This phenomenon was brought on by the Internet, of course, an amazing creation that seemed to come out of nowhere and that everyone thought would hold the key to great wealth even if they couldn't quite figure out how that would happen. So they started flinging business plans against the wall to see which ones would stick. And it got so it didn't even matter if they didn't stick because there was plenty of venture capital to fund even the half-baked ideas. Once Netscape went public in 1995 and saw its share price rise from $28 to $58 on the first day of trading, venture capitalists saw that they could pour money into unprofitable enterprises and, if the concept had enough sizzle, be assured of their ability to unload stock on eager investors and make an enormous profit. And thus began the initial public offering (IPO) boom that has made billionaires out of what appear to me to be little kids.

Fortune magazine has a list of "40 under 40" that is the younger generation's equivalent of Forbes's richest Americans list. In 2000, the list contained 13 billionaires: The top three were Michael Dell, chairman and CEO of Dell Computer, with $17 billion; Ted Waitt, chairman and CEO of Gateway, with $8 billion; and David Filo, "chief Yahoo" and co-founder of Yahoo! with $6 billion. The rest of the 2000 billionaires had titles like chairman, CEO, and founder of companies like Amazon.com, eBay, Real-Networks, Quest Software, Blue Martini Software, and Sapient. All were in their 30s; all were worth more than a billion dollars; and all are smart, savvy entrepreneurs who managed to convert big ideas into actual wealth—at least on paper.

In its September 18, 2000, issue *Fortune* noted that the list changed substantially from the year before. In fact more than half of the executives that made the 1999 list had dropped off the list in 2000. Specifically:

> Nearly a third of last year's winners were bumped by the market's springtime hurricane, which ravaged the wealth of earnings-challenged, consumer-focused dot-coms. Thus, Scott Blum of Buy.com is gone, $1.2 billion poorer than last year. So is Jeff Arnold of WebMD, who is $181 million lighter, and Toby Lenk of e-Toys, who saw $235 million of his net worth vaporize. In their place are the founders and CEOs of the current hot sectors of the tech market: Internet infrastructure and broadband.

Fortune's analysis of what it took for the "40 under 40" to get rich?

> Drive had something to do with it, and salesmanship. Deep engineering skills played a part for some members. But the attributes that figure in almost everyone's story are timing and foresight. Nothing in the history of American enterprise has paid off quite as well as being the first to perceive (and act on) trends in the whirlwind evolution of digital technology, especially the Internet.

And what about next year's list? Well, it will be different.

Indeed, it's this temporary nature of today's wealth that has people in a frenzy to grab whatever they can: to secure the stock options, exercise them, sell the stock, and get the money into the bank before Wall Street figures out what the stock is really worth. The game is changing by the minute, and as this book is being written it looks as if profits are starting to matter again. During speculative frenzies, when prices are rising *just because* prices are rising, you can make money on anything: baseball cards, tulips, unprofitable companies. It's called the greater fool theory. Meanwhile, serious investors like Warren Buffett refuse to take part because they don't understand the basis that is being used to value stocks. (In reality, there is no basis, just the belief that someone else will be willing to pay more.) When the last fool has gotten in, the market collapses, the speculators leave, and the serious investors sift through the rubble for bargains.

This is not to say that opportunities to amass great wealth have disappeared. Far from it. The opportunities that await those who can see into the future and create something that's unique, powerful, and life-changing are more abundant than ever. But maybe the goal should not be to get rich, but rather to leave a mark on society. To find your calling and run with it. If that leads you to billionairedom, great. You'll never have to worry about money again (you'll probably have lots of other worries, though).

But you can get the same effect with far less money and have a more balanced life in the process. Most people want to have it all—not all the money, but all the rich rewards life has to offer such as meaningful work, satisfying relationships, and freedom from worry. It takes a certain amount of money to achieve that last goal—that's what the rest of this book is about—but we'd probably be wise to shift our sights from building great wealth to building a happy life. That's what many of my clients have done, and I'd like to suggest that these mere millionaires may serve as better role models than the billionaires profiled in this chapter.

CHAPTER THREE

HOW RICH DO YOU WANT TO BE?

Wealth is a means to an end, not the end itself. As a synonym for health and happiness, it has had a fair trial and failed dismally.

John Galsworthy

HOW RICH DO YOU REALLY WANT TO BE? Are you driven to amass great wealth, or do you just want a comfortable life? You may be on a mission to make a lot of money right now, and that's fine. Sometimes the focused pursuit of wealth is absolutely the right thing to do, even if it comes at the expense of a balanced life . . . as long as it's viewed as a temporary endeavor. However, most rich, driven people usually stop at some point in their lives and ask themselves, "What's it all for?" The tragedy is when this moment of reflection comes late in life, after marriages have failed and neglected children have spent a fortune on therapists.

DOES MONEY BUY HAPPINESS?

Let's think about why you might want to get rich in the first place. Is it a certain amount of money that you want, or just a comfortable life? Are you feeling stressed about money, or the lack of it, and what you really want is to get rid of the stress? Do you feel locked in a job or living situation that, but for the money, you would be free to leave? I have a feeling that most people who say they want to strike it rich aren't after the money but a style of life that isn't even all that lavish. Maybe a newer car and a bigger house in a nicer neighborhood. A vacation once or twice a year. The ability to dine in nice restaurants whenever they feel like it and to order a good bottle of wine without having to watch every penny.

But these things don't require great wealth. Not the Bill Gates kind of wealth. Not the kind of wealth that makes people crazy with envy when they read about the lucky ones who have cashed in hundreds of millions of dollars worth of stock options. Not the kind of wealth that makes people squander their money on lottery tickets in an attempt to win huge jackpots. If you were to make a list of all the things you wanted, I'll bet you'd find the total to be surprisingly low. It wouldn't come anywhere near a billion dollars. It wouldn't be $100 million or even $10 million. Think about it. If you had $10 million, you could put it into tax-free municipal bonds at 4 percent interest and have an annual income of $400,000 for life. That's $33,333 per month. After tax. Could you even spend that much? Now, I'm not suggesting that 4 percent municipal bonds would necessarily be a good investment for someone with $10 million, because it doesn't give the capital an opportunity to grow. I have found that once wealthy individuals have more money than they need to maintain the lifestyle they desire, they want to deploy that capital in a way that will keep it growing, for their children and grandchildren or for their favorite charities. As a matter of fact, it's this attitude that money is something to be preserved and invested, not spent, that has enabled many of my clients to get rich in the first place.

The point I'm trying to make is that it doesn't make sense to set your sights on some astronomical figure if you can't make it relate to your own life. The goal must be real to you. This doesn't mean you should necessarily set your sights low—if you're bound and determined to accumulate $10 million, more power to you. But if maintaining an unrealistic goal is causing you to do stupid things like buy lottery tickets, I suggest that you approach goal setting from a different perspective and determine how much money you really need based on the kind of life you want to have. This chapter will help you do that.

The question is how money can change the quality of your life, which is really what most people mean when they say they want the big bucks. They want the freedom to leave a job they hate, perhaps to change careers or start a business doing something they've always wanted to do. They want to spend more time with their family. They want to raise their children in a safe, comfortable environment and provide them with a good education. They want to be able to retire someday without being dependent on family. They want to do good works in the community and have enough money that they can give to others without it hurting their own pocketbook. These are the things my clients tell me they want when they ask for help setting up a plan for saving and investing.

That's the other thing to keep in mind about goal setting. Great wealth doesn't happen all at once. (Yes, yes, I know it can, if you inherit money or hit the lottery jackpot. But since you can't count on those things happening, the only sure way to accumulate money is to work, save, and invest. I may be saying this a few more times before this book is finished.) Since life unfolds day by day, the money you need to live this ever-evolving drama comes to you gradually, in installments, whether by regular paycheck, revenues to a business, annual investment returns, or periodic windfalls. Hardly anybody starts out life with all the money they'll need for the rest of their life. It just doesn't work that way. Indeed, the honest earning of money, however one chooses to do it, is a very important part of living a life. As much as we'd like to think we could have a better life if we never had to worry about money again, the truth is that the act of making money often defines our lives.

In the book *The Virtue of Prosperity* (The Free Press, 2000, p. 125), Dinesh D'Souza tells the story of T. J. Rodgers, the chief executive officer (CEO) of Cypress Semiconductor. Rodgers was approached about running for Congress. He said, "No way could I do that. We make chips with over ten million transistors on them. And we pay $100 million a year to our people, which supports a whole lot of families, houses, cars, college educations, what have you. That's more good than any congressman does, ever. So for me to go from wealth creator to wealth distributor, I would become depressed, probably suicidal." He goes on to say, "Money is not my prime motivator. But that's only because I have as much money as I'll ever need. So what drives me now is winning a difficult competition, reaching my goals for success, and learning."

In other words, he is operating within our capitalist system to achieve a variety of goals, both financial and nonfinancial. That's what we all do when we go to work everyday. We may think we're working only for the money, but if we really think about it, we get far more from our jobs than a paycheck. Our jobs give us a chance to make a difference in people's lives, even if our role is just one small part in a cast of thousands. Our work gives us an opportunity to interact with other people, to learn from them, and to share our insights with others who, unbeknownst to us, may be tremendously influenced by our presence in their lives. If you're saying, "Oh, no, I hate my job and if I didn't have to work I'd quit in a heartbeat," then you're in the wrong job.

Many of the Silicon Valley millionaires you've read about and envied have not used their wealth to retire from the work-force. An article in the *San Jose Mercury News* (Nov. 2, 2000) titled "Why Valley Workers Take the Money and Don't Run" re-ported why wealth doesn't mean retirement for many high-tech workers. They don't leave because they love what they do. They like being around smart, stimulating people; they like working on challenging projects; they like building and creating. I also have personal experience with this. I've been fortunate enough in my own career and my investments to retire now if I wanted to, but I'm having too much fun in my job, meeting new people and helping them achieve financial security. If you're stuck in a job you hate, the solution may not be permanent retirement to a lake in Montana, but a different job that makes you feel stimu-lated, happy, and useful. The freedom to change jobs is a very real financial goal—and a very popular one among today's stressed-out workers. I'll be talking more about this subject in Chapter 4.

HOW TO SET FINANCIAL GOALS

As a financial advisor, one of my roles is to help people set fi-nancial goals. This means helping them determine how much money they'll need and when. Sometimes this is strictly a num-bers exercise. For example, if a husband and wife say they have two kids ages 8 and 10 and they want to send them to the best private university in the country when they graduate from high school, all I have to do is plug in the numbers for today's costs, add in an inflation factor for the number of years remaining until each child reaches age 18, multiply it times 4 years of college, multiply it times 2 kids, and we have our financial goal. Anyone can do this. There are even calculators on the Web that enable you to skip some of these steps. For example, at www.finaid.org, you can simply enter today's cost for 1 year of college (it even tells you that the average cost is $10,458 for public universities and $22,533 for private universities), an estimated inflation rate, and the number of years until the child starts college. The calculator figures the cost for each of the 4 years of college and comes up with a grand total.

This numbers-crunching kind of goal setting is easy (except when my clients fall off their chairs upon hearing the number. In the example above, the grand total would be $157,110 for the 10-year-old and $176,529 for the 8-year-old, or $333,639 for both.) Sometimes we have to discuss priorities: Do they want to scale back the goal and perhaps send the children to a public university? Or would they rather make a few sacrifices in their present lifestyle in order to increase their savings? Goal setting is all about establishing priorities and making decisions about how you want to live your life. It's really about life planning. Finances are just a part of it.

WHY PLAN?

Why should we engage in life planning? Why not just live in the moment and enjoy our money as it flows to us throughout our lifetimes? Well, certain things in life require more than one month's salary. And paying for them after the fact doesn't work so well either. Commercialism and credit cards have formed terrible habits in the American people. They make us want things, and then they show us how easy it is to get them. Buy now, pay later. Then, of course, we're paying interest on top of the cost of the item we couldn't afford to buy in the first place. And because we're making payments every month on things we may not even own anymore (or experiences long forgotten), we can't afford to save for the future. It's a vicious spiral, and if you are presently caught in it you have my greatest sympathy and support. Although it can seem like a never-ending conundrum, many people have managed to get out of debt by cutting their spending and chipping away at the mountain of debt until it's all gone. Credit counseling may help. If you are feeling stuck, if you feel your debts are keeping you from moving on with your life, call the Consumer Credit Counseling service in your area. (Don't fall for any of the credit repair schemes you see advertised; Consumer Credit Counseling Service is a nonprofit organization that is free or has only a nominal fee and has had great success helping people get out of debt.) Sometimes just picking up the phone is all the action it takes to turn your life around. Meanwhile, continue with this goal-setting exercise, and make getting out of debt just one of your many goals. Seeing it in that light may help put it in perspective and remove any negative feelings you have associated with it.

Next on the goal list is the establishment of an emergency fund. This, of course, acknowledges that life planning is only so effective. If we could plan our lives down to the letter, all of our goals would be provided for and we'd have no need for an emergency fund. But as you know, stuff happens. Layoffs occur. Illness hits. Transmissions die. Teeth hurt. For these unexpected expenses you need funds liquid and available so you don't have to borrow or dip into your long-term investment accounts. I recommend having 3 to 6 months' living expenses set aside as an emergency fund. By the way, emergencies don't always have to be bad. One of my clients, a successful ad executive, became good friends with a chef and decided at the age of 45 to partner with him and buy a restaurant. This enterprise required a chunk of cash that he hadn't planned on needing, but it was an opportunity to spice up his life, so to speak, and have some fun with a midlife business venture. If the whole idea of an emergency fund seems too negative for you, put a positive spin on it instead. Think of it as a cash reserve for unexpected investment or business opportunities. (If you do use the money for that purpose—or any other, for that matter—be sure to replenish the fund as soon as you can.)

IMAGINING YOUR FUTURE

For the rest of your life planning, start imagining your future the way you would like it to play out. Do this in whatever way works for you. Some people go to the beach or take a walk and mentally run through their ideal life as if it were a movie. Others sit down with a piece of paper and make notes: age 30, buy a house; age 35, start a family; age 53, send kids to college; age 65, retire. Some people plan the next 5 or 10 years in meticulous detail—planning for new cars, weddings and vacations down to the penny (as Figure 3-1 will help you do)—while leaving retirement and other major late-in-life plans somewhat sketchy and subject to change (but still setting aside a portion of their salary to cover them).

If you have difficulty visualizing future events—and many people do—it may help to talk to someone. One of my clients who was forced into early retirement thought that he'd like to move to Las Vegas from Los Angeles, where he'd lived most of his life. He thought it made sense from a financial standpoint because housing costs were lower and Nevada has no state income tax. But as we started talking about it, and as I asked him questions about where his children lived and what his life in Las Vegas might be like, he began to see that it might be a lonely existence in a new city and harder than he thought to pull himself away from the community he'd lived in for so long. He had started the whole discussion by asking me how much of a down payment he should put on a new house in Vegas. When I recommended that he rent for awhile first to make sure he would like it, he started thinking about the impact such a move might have on his overall happiness, particularly being away from family and friends he'd known for years. In the end, he decided to stay in L.A. I'm not positive about this, but I may have saved a retired gentleman the pain of loneliness in his old age, simply by helping him visualize his future in a way that went beyond his pocketbook. I've seen too many retirees pick up stakes and move from one part of the country to another and find themselves miserable, even though the move might have made sense from an economic standpoint.

THE MYSTERY OF LIFE

You may be at a stage in life where lots of things are up for grabs. You're single but hope to get married someday. You're childless and haven't decided yet if you want to have children. You're in the beginning stages of a career and aren't sure if you'll stick with it or go back to school and head in another direction. You're in an unhappy marriage and aren't sure what to do about it. You've been wanting to pursue a career in the arts but haven't figured out how to make the transition. Your whole life isn't what you'd like it to be and you'd love to get a fresh start somehow.

When your life is in a state of flux, it can be difficult to set concrete financial goals. How can you plan for a future that's so murky? How can you know how much money you'll need when you don't even know what you'd be spending it on? Valid points, but dangerous. For one thing, nobody knows exactly how life will unfold. Some people have a better handle on it than others, but even the most focused among us get blindsided at times, by falling in love, getting pregnant, or meeting the one person who can launch their career in a whole new direction. So take it as fact that life is meant to be a mystery. Nobody has all the answers. And that's the way it should be.

But if you feel yourself drifting and would like to become more focused, financial planning can actually help you find direction. We live in a time when our options are limitless. We can do anything, be anything, have anything we want. All these options give us the opportunity to shape our lives in any way we want, but they can also create tremendous confusion and anxiety. What if we choose wrong? What if we pick one option, change our mind and go with a different one, and then realize that we'd have been better off if we'd stuck with the first one? We find ourselves drifting simply because there are too many choices.

Financial planning forces you to make assumptions. You're not making life choices, really, because you know that things could change. But because you don't want to find yourself at age 65 with nothing saved for retirement, for example, you assume that you'll retire at age 65, even knowing full well that you may want to keep working longer or with luck may be able to retire earlier than that. A good example of how assumptions do not constitute life choices is the case of a young single woman, 30 years old, happy in her career, who would marry if the right man came along. She can't exactly start planning for babies and family expenses as if she were part of a couple because she doesn't know when, or even if, she will marry. So for financial planning purposes she assumes she will stay single and be responsible for taking care of herself. She contributes to her retirement plan, sets near-term financial goals such as periodic vacations, and starts saving for a down payment on a house. If she does meet the man of her dreams, none of these financial planning activities will have been wasted. She will be that much further ahead and will have the pleasure of being able to bring financial assets into the marriage. Once she and her new husband tie the knot, she can change some of her assumptions and they can chart a new financial course as a couple. And if the marriage should end—and you know, all marriages do end at some point, through death if not divorce—she'll have her retirement taken care of and won't have to join the ranks of poverty-stricken widows who always thought someone would be around to take care of them.

DEALING WITH LARGE NUMBERS

What if you go through this exercise, listing your goals and quantifying them using Figure 3-1, and the numbers blow you away? What if you discover that with a house, a couple of kids, college, retirement, and a few vacations—nothing out of the ordinary in American life today—you're going to need $2 million? Wherever will you get that kind of money? It's enough to make you tear up the paper, throw up your hands, and console yourself with a bottle of cheap wine. You must prepare yourself for large numbers and remember what I said about not needing the money all at once. You don't have to have the whole $2 million by a certain date. It's a lifelong process. You'd be amazed how much money will come to you over your lifetime, both from working and

Figure 3-1   Goal worksheet.

Goal	Amount Needed	Date Needed	Priority (1, 2, 3)
Get out of debt			1
Establish an emergency fund			1
Start a family			
Buy a house			
Start a business			
Send kids to college			
Redecorate the house			
Major home maintenance items (paint, roof)			
Take a vacation			
Buy a car			
Buy a boat			
Buy a second home			
Finance a fancy wedding			
Go back to school			
Take a sabbatical			
Amass $_____ by _____			

investment returns on your savings. Because it comes to you in dribs and drabs, and because you're probably spending it as fast as it comes in (I hope this book makes you rethink that nasty little habit), you aren't aware of the grand total of all the money that comes to you over your lifetime.

Let's say you start working at age 22 earning a salary of $25,000. As you progress up the career ladder, your income rises by 5 percent a year. This increase represents merit raises only, not inflation. (I've found that people have a hard enough time dealing with large numbers without putting the inflation factor into it. We deal with inflation later, by assuming your raises will also include a cost-of-living factor on top of the merit raises and by making sure investment returns exceed the inflation rate.) So when you're 23 you'll be making $26,250, at 24 you'll be making $27,562, and so on. By age 62, your annual salary will be $167,518. If you were to add up your salary for all of the years, you would find that over your 40-year career you would have earned a grand total of $2,992,882. Now, if you had also managed to save 10 percent of your salary every year and earned average investment returns of 8 percent, you would accumulate an additional $1,007,555 in investment returns alone. That's a total of more than $4 million dollars that would have come into your possession over your 40-year working lifetime. Now, what you do with all that money is your business. Helping you see why it makes sense not to squander every penny the minute it comes into your possession is mine. By doing a little financial planning, you can spread out your expenses and save up for the big stuff so you won't find yourself out of money when college tuition bills come due and retirement looms.

Here's another reason to do financial planning: If you're a pessimist it can help you relax. Some of my clients have it in their minds that college for two kids will cost $500,000 and retirement will require millions and millions. The media and the mutual fund companies have done such a good job of scaring people into thinking that inflation will continue to drive up the already high cost of living that some of my conservative clients are afraid to spend a penny. They deprive themselves today thinking they'll need the money tomorrow. By running the numbers and showing them what they'll need versus what they can be expected to have, they often find that they can breathe easier.

The important thing to remember when dealing with large numbers is that as long as you're working, saving, and investing, you will have a constant flow of cash coming into your life. It's even possible that by the time your kids go to college, you'll be so far along in your career and have such a high income that you'll easily be able to afford tuition payments out of your regular take-home pay. This is the case for several of my high-income clients who have built successful careers. I wouldn't necessarily recommend counting on this, though, because college costs are already quite high and have been rising at a rate of 5 to 6 percent a year. Also, in today's knowledge-based economy a college education is more important than ever. It's really too important a goal to leave to chance. But if you do get spooked by the big numbers that pop up once you've written down your goals and quantified them, just remember that your income-earning years are far from over.

HOW FLEXIBLE ARE YOUR GOALS?

Planning for a one-time future expenditure is easy. For example, if you want to take a European vacation in 2 years at an estimated cost of $10,000, any planning calculator will show you that you need to save $393 per month over the 2 years, assuming an annual compound return of 6 percent. (The shorter the goal, the more conservative the investments should be; that's why I used 6 percent in this example and not the usual 8 percent, which is appropriate for long-term goals.) You can use this method of calculation for any goal that represents a fixed amount of money that must be available on a specific date. Examples include a down payment on a house; the purchase of a car, boat, couch, diamond ring, or other expensive item; a wedding or other fancy shindig; college tuition.

Sometimes you have flexibility in setting certain goals, and again this is where assumptions come in. No, you don't *have* to go to Europe in 2 years, but if you set it as a goal and then assume that the goal will be met, you can start setting the necessary savings aside and begin collecting travel brochures. In this way financial planning allows you to have the things you want. If you're lamenting that you never go on vacation, maybe it's because you've never planned for it. In the case of a vacation, you're taking something that's completely optional and turning it into a must-have (or certainly a want-to-have). Certain other goals already are must-haves and therefore do not offer as much flexibility (nor are they as much fun to save for). When the roof on your house wears out, you'll need to replace it. Not much flexibility there. Some goals are a necessary part of life and offer little choice in when they must be met, but others are completely optional and if you don't cast them in semistone you'll never realize them. Above all, don't ever forget that you're here to have fun. Financial responsibility need not get in the way of enjoying life. In fact, it can help you enjoy it more!

One set of decisions has to do with setting the goal—which goals to set, how much money you'll need for each goal, and when you'd like for the goal to be achieved. Another consideration is how important it is to reach the goal. Some goals offer little leeway. For example, once the roof starts going, you may be able to patch it for a couple of years, but at some point you'll need to replace it. The cost will be somewhat variable depending on the type of shingles you select, but you probably won't get away for less than $20,000. In this case you have only a little flexibility with regard to *when* and *how much*, and no flexibility at all with regard to *if* (as long as you plan to stay in the house). For a goal of this nature you'll need to make sure you stay on track with your saving and investing because the risks of not attaining the goal are too high—a collapsed roof or the added interest expense if you have to incur debt to replace it.

The European vacation, however, offers lots of flexibility as to when, how much, and even if it is ultimately realized. Although it would be disappointing if your plans somehow went awry, it would not be a catastrophe to have to postpone the vacation or spend less than you had planned. When saving and investing for any goal, you'll need to look at how much flexibility is associated with the goal and plan accordingly. Keep this in mind when you get to the investing part of financial planning (Chapters 6, 7, and 8). Once you've set a goal and established a savings plan, you'll want to invest the funds in a way that's consistent with the amount of flexibility you have. Your time horizon has a lot to do with how you choose to invest.

A NEW WAY TO LOOK AT RISK

In the investment business we talk about risk. Usually risk refers to volatility, or the degree to which an investment portfolio fluctuates in value as securities prices move up and down. But in real life, risk has to do with the chance of not achieving your goal. If you invest your European vacation funds in stocks hoping to earn the long-term historical *average* rate of 11 percent, you could be unpleasantly surprised when returns for stocks over the 2 years *you* own them are below average. In other words, your stocks could be down in value right around the time you were planning to buy your airplane tickets. The stock market (as measured by the S&P 500, Standard & Poor's index of the 500 largest companies in the United States) has had 11 down years since 1950. If you had left your money invested all that time, you would have earned a positive annual return averaging 11 percent. But if you'd started saving on January 1, 1973 hoping to go to Europe on December 31, 1974, you probably would have ended up staying home because the market was down 14 percent and 26 percent respectively, in those 2 years (the worst 2 years out of the last 50).

Understanding the amount of flexibility you have with regard to any particular goal is essential. If you are determined to go to Europe 2 years hence, and if you are not willing to sacrifice the amount of time spent there or the lavishness of the accommodations, you'd be wise to put your savings into an investment that does not fluctuate in value.

Long-term goals are different, however. In fact, you must reverse your thinking on long-term goals, because while you sleep inflation will be bumping up your goal ever so slightly. When you wake up in 30 years you'll find that you need much more than you ever thought you would. Do you remember when movies cost a couple of bucks, a two-bedroom apartment rented for $250, and you could buy a new car for $5,000? Anyone who was establishing retirement goals back then figured they could live comfortably on $1,200 per month. Thirty years later, they wake up and find that they need more than $5,000 to maintain the same standard of living. If you'd told them back then that their $250-per-month apartment would one day rent for $1,100, they would have said you were crazy; they couldn't imagine anyone spending that much for a dinky little apartment. So when I tell you that if inflation averages just 4 percent a year over the next 30 years, today's $1,100-per-month apartment will cost more than $3,600 per month, you'll probably say, "Get outta here! Whoever would pay that much for a dinky little apartment?" That's why I don't like to use inflation-adjusted dollars when setting long-term goals; people just don't believe them. But get this: if it costs you $5,000 per month to live now, and if inflation averages 4 percent, it will cost you $16,500 per month in 30 years. That's without increasing your standard of living and assuming the cost of everything you buy goes up by 4 percent a year. And as you've probably noticed at the pharmacy and in the movie ticket line, lots of things go up faster than the general inflation rate.

The only way to achieve your long-term goals is to earn a rate of return that's higher than the inflation rate. Otherwise you're going backward. And because your long-term goals give you some flexibility as to when you'll need to liquidate your investments, you don't have to worry about selling your stocks when they're down. A good rule of thumb is to keep any funds you'll need in the next 5 years in a money market fund or short-term bond fund. Beyond 5 years, you can invest in stocks. More on this in Chapter 7.

PLANNING FOR ONGOING EXPENSES

As just noted, planning for a one-time expense is easy. Just decide how much money you'll need, when you'll need it, and how much you need to save based on an assumed rate of return. But what if you want to take a European vacation not once, but every year? What if you not only want to send your kids to the best university in the country, but to the best private school in your city, starting in kindergarten? What if you want to retire someday with an income of $5,000 every month (in today's dollars)? These goals require an ongoing income stream that must come from somewhere.

There are two ways to create an income stream. One is to work for it. The other is to compile a lump sum of money from which you can withdraw the amount you need while the rest of it keeps growing. Your near-term goals, like private school for the kids, will likely come from your own labor, while the long-term ones, like retirement, will come from the lump sum you have so diligently saved over the years. Where all this gets tricky is when you try to balance all the goals. What you *don't* want to do is spend so much on private schools and other near-term goals that you don't have any money left at the end of each month to save for the long-term goals. *All important goals must be saved for simultaneously, not sequentially*. If you were to wait until the kids were through college before starting to save for retirement, you'd find it very difficult to accumulate the amount needed in such a short time.

Therefore it's important to look at your life as a continuum, starting at birth and ending at death, and understand not only where you are on the continuum, but also try to get a clear picture of the part of the continuum that you haven't lived yet—the future. And although nobody knows exactly where the continuum will end, the mystery of when you'll exit this Earth shouldn't stop you from planning. Generations ago, people just assumed they'd die within a few years after retiring. We can't assume that anymore. And as much as we may love our work and swear we'll never retire, there will likely come a point when we simply can't work anymore. We should at least give ourselves the luxury of

deciding whether we want to keep working or pack it in for a life
of leisure. Who knows how we'll feel at age 70, after we've spent
a good 40 or 50 years in the work force?

RETIREMENT COMES FIRST

Even though retirement comes last in life, it should be saved for
first, because it will take an awful lot of money to fund several
decades of living expenses. The only way to get there is to start
saving early to get the seed money growing and compounding so
that eventually it takes on a life of its own. In the later years the
investment earnings will comprise a far bigger portion of the
fund than the savings you put into it.

Let's take the previous example, where we assume you start
earning $25,000 per year at age 22, that your salary increases 5
percent a year, and that you save 10 percent of your salary every
year and invest it at 8 percent. In the first year, your savings
amount will be $2,500 (10% × $25,000) and your investment
earnings will be $200 ($2,500 × 8%). This first year, your hard-
earned savings obviously represent the biggest chunk of the still
meager retirement fund. But guess what happens in the 40th year?
The situation is vastly reversed. Your annual savings amount is
$16,752 (10% of your now $167,520 salary), but your investment
return in the 40th year is a whopping $97,658. That's because by
this time, your retirement fund has grown to $1,220,732. And
8 percent of $1,220,732 is $97,658, giving you a grand total of
$1,318,390 at the end of the 40th year.

Want to know how much income this investment will yield
if you decide to retire at age 62? Assuming you earn investment
returns of 7 percent throughout retirement, you can withdraw
$8,720 per month before exhausting the fund at age 92. That's
equivalent to $1,771 in today's dollars, assuming 4 percent infla-
tion. If you'd like to play around with the numbers yourself, go to
www.timevalue.com and enter the variables it asks for.

Now, we still haven't covered all the bases here, because the
amount you start withdrawing at 62 will not be enough at 92. If
it takes $8,720 to meet your living expenses in your first year of

retirement, it will take $29,000 per month in your last year of re-
tirement, assuming a 4 percent inflation rate. See what I mean
about the numbers becoming ridiculously impossible to deal
with? If you're 22 now, it's pointless to try to predict how much
money it will take for you to live 70 years from now. Who
knows . . . by then we may all be living on a space station and
talking about that quaint concept called money, which was out-
moded back in 2050.

Here's how we deal with retirement savings when all attempts at estimating a precise future goal result in the fear of big
numbers and frustration that the goal keeps growing larger than
your ability to keep up with it: Choose some percentage of your
salary, say 5 or 10 percent, and commit to saving that amount
every year. Don't think about it, just do it. Don't worry if it's
enough. It probably is, as long as your salary increases over your
working lifetime and you keep up the habit of saving and don't
dip into it for things like European vacations and new roofs for
the house.

As you grow older and closer to your retirement goal, you
can begin to play around with actual numbers to see if you're on
track. Somewhere in your 40s is the time to take stock of how
much you have and compare it to how much you think you'll
need. If you're afraid of coming up short, you can bump up your
savings or aim for higher investment returns. In your 50s, same
thing but with even greater accuracy in the numbers. Now you
can begin to consider other sources of income, such as Social Security and, if you feel like it, part-time work. This may take the
pressure off somewhat and show you that you are indeed on
track for your retirement goals. I'll be talking more about retirement savings vehicles in Chapter 5.

PRIORITIZING YOUR OTHER GOALS

Once your retirement savings plan is in place, you can begin to
concentrate on other goals. A worksheet (Figure 3-1) can help
you get started. Please note: It's very important not to become

overwhelmed by this goal-setting process. You may find that you want far more than your present income will allow you to have. Do not let this disparity discourage you from planning your financial future! And definitely don't use it as an excuse to buy lottery tickets. Use it instead to motivate you to work harder, advance in your career, save more, and invest wisely.

Prioritize your goals. Decide which ones are most important and which ones are not essential but would be nice to have. Integrate your goal setting with your budget so you can make those agonizing decisions about whether to dine out this week or save the money for a summer vacation. Remember, this is your life, and only you can decide what you want to do with your money. I'm just trying to combat the enormous influence the credit card companies have had in making us think we can have it all now without any sacrifice. It all comes down to this: Earn more or spend less. If you're tired of the rat race and opt for a life of voluntary simplicity, you'll want to focus on the spend less option. Still, you may be surprised by how little effort it takes to earn more—whether through smart career choices or savvy investing. That's what the rest of this book is about.

CHAPTER FOUR

MAKING MONEY THE OLD-FASHIONED WAY

If hard work is the key to success, most people would rather pick the lock.

Claude McDonald

WHATEVER HAPPENED TO THAT QUAINT IDEA of working for a living? Our fathers and grandfathers used to do it without question. They went to the office or the plant every day around eight or nine and came home around five or six, and every 2 weeks brought home a paycheck. Work was work, and very few people questioned whether it should be "meaningful" or "fulfilling" or "challenging." Indeed, those who had heard stories of the Great Depression from their parents (or remembered living through it as children) saw work as a privilege in its own right. The idea of earning an honest day's pay for an honest day's work held great value during mid-20th century America.

In most people's minds, there was no other way to make money. Sure, everyone knew about the wealthy business titans like J. D. Rockefeller and J. P. Morgan, but those avenues to wealth certainly didn't seem open to the average person. So they did what they assumed everyone had to do to make ends meet: They worked every day of their lives, starting in their 20s and ending, usually, in their 60s. No questions asked. Job stability was highly valued. More than four or five job changes in a lifetime was looked upon with suspicion, so people generally stayed put, advancing up the career ladder in a fairly steady progression until it was time to retire. Then they would start receiving a monthly pension check that was guaranteed for life. That, along with Social Security and a little savings, enabled them to live comfortably in retirement until it was time to go.

Those of us today who are on a fast track to make money look at the Organization Man of the 1950s and wonder how he could have lived that way. (The term *Organization Man* came from the title of a book written by William Hollingworth Whyte in the 1950s, in which he chronicled the life of a man who stayed with the organization.) An easy job with a steady paycheck that never changed except for small raises every year? Talk about a slacker! Where's his ambition? Where's his get-up-and-go? He may have been satisfied with a tract house in the suburbs and a new Chevrolet every 5 years, but we want more. We want challenge, excitement, and most of all—lots and lots of money. And as soon as we get it, we're going to blow this work gig and kick back and enjoy life. Life's too short to spend everyday going to work!

FINANCIAL PLANNING WAS EASIER BACK THEN

Before I focus on the realities of life and work and money, I'd like to talk about a very important phenomenon that went along with the Organization Man's steady, stable lifestyle. Because he couldn't count on stock options or big year-end bonuses, he disciplined himself to plan ahead and to save for the things his family needed. There were no credit cards in those days. The only things people went into debt for were their houses and maybe their cars. When they went out to dinner they paid cash. When they went on vacation they wrote checks for their airline tickets (unless they went by car, which was common) and took enough cash to cover lodging and meals (there were no automatic teller machines). They set money aside for their children's college educations and for any other expenses that were likely to come up, such as a new water heater or a new lawn mower. Banks offered Christmas clubs to encourage people to put $25 or $50 a month into a special account for Christmas. If they wanted to buy something they couldn't afford such as a new refrigerator, they often put it on layaway, making small monthly payments until it was all paid off. Only then could they take the item home.

In some ways financial planning was easier then, because people knew exactly what they had to work with. The biweekly paychecks were predictable. The monthly fixed expenses such as mortgage payments, utilities, and food were predictable. And when it came to planning vacations or other large expenses, the family would gather around the kitchen table and make decisions about what they could buy and do based on how much extra money was available. Then they made the commitment to set that money aside and relished the anticipation of growing closer to their goal.

As much as we may want to, there are several reasons why we can't go back to that exact way of living. For one thing, the business world is changing so fast that companies no longer tolerate an employee who learns one set of skills early in life and expects to coast on those same skills for the rest of his or her career. People today must manage their careers, constantly updating their skills and working to get ahead. I have a feeling the reason so many people want to make a quick fortune and get out of the workforce is that this idea of constant change is very unsettling for them. They can't imagine what the work world will be like in 10 years, so they simply decide not to be a part of it. The other reason people want to make their money and run is that many jobs are highly stressful these days. They involve long hours, tiresome commutes, and interactions with clients or other employees that are competitive and very stressful. No one can sustain a high flow of adrenalin for very long; even cavemen could relax after the big kill and munch on a large animal for awhile until it was time to gear up for another battle. The stress level has reached the point where people are looking longingly at jobs like teaching, writing, or running a small business and thinking seriously about a major career change. But since these jobs don't pay very much, they want to make a bunch of money very fast so they can have it all—a low-stress job *and* an upper-middle-class lifestyle.

Another reason we can't go back to the old way is that household economics have changed. Everything is so much more expensive today! When I went to college at Northwestern University in the 1970s, one year's tuition was $6,000. Today it's $25,839. My parents paid for my education in full without it being a tremendous strain on their pocketbook. Today, it's nearly impossible for a family to finance a full 4 years of college for 1 or 2 kids without loans, grants, and serious planning and saving. The government tells us inflation has been under control for several decades, with price increases averaging 3 to 4 percent a year.

Well, these increases add up. And some expenses, like health care, have gone up much faster than the rate of inflation. Health insurance alone puts such a strain on some families' budgets that there's little left to save for vacations or anything else. So out come the credit cards.

In some respects, we can and should go back to the old ways, but we need to adapt those ways to a new world. We seem to have lost our center when it comes to personal finance. Unpredictable career paths mean we never know exactly how much money will be coming in, making it very hard to plan. Widespread advertising and easy credit have made it so we can't even tell if we can afford something or not. So we close our eyes, stick out the card, and hope for the best. What we really need to do is go back to the kitchen table and plan. Prices may be higher now, and we may not know exactly how much money we have to work with, but we must get a handle on our finances, live within our means, make decisions about what we want to buy and do with our money, and set the necessary funds aside ahead of time. This allows us to earn interest on our money and build the pot faster, rather than buying things first and then *paying* interest on borrowed funds if we charge it. Buy-now-pay-later may have made sense during a very brief time in the 1970s when prices were rising at a faster rate than interest rates: Back then, if you waited to buy something you might end up paying more than it would cost you in interest to charge it. That's not the case today and hasn't been for some time. If you charge a $10,000 purchase at 18 percent interest and make the 2 percent minimum payment every month, it will take you 57 years and 7 months to repay the debt and cost you a total of $28,931 in interest.

MANAGING YOUR CAREER

If you want to make your money fast so you can exit the high-pressure work world, you will need to manage your career somewhat differently from the person who believes work offers an opportunity for fun and challenge and is in it for the long haul. You both may have something to learn from the two strategies, however.

If you plan to work for many decades, you run the risk of becoming complacent in your career. Without the carrot of earning a large fortune and then being able to enjoy a life of leisure (or whatever), you may end up plodding along, missing out on opportunities to advance in your career, and failing to earn as much as you otherwise might be able to. But, if you're in a hurry to get in and get out after making your many millions, you run the risk of making some serious career missteps, such as leaving a good job with an established company for a shaky startup that's in danger of going under and missing out on some valuable mentoring or career experience. The guidelines that follow are directed to both of you. I'm hoping that people who have a tendency toward complacency in their careers will be inspired to move ahead, while the go-getters who want to get rich quick because they think work is terrible will find that a well-managed career really can be a rewarding part of life.

CONSIDER YOUR LIFETIME EARNINGS

When contemplating careers and job opportunities, most of us look at how much we can make in one year in salary and benefits. Seldom do we map out potential earnings over our working lifetime and strategize ways to maximize those earnings. Just as we did in goal setting in Chapter 3, we should view our lives as a continuum. By knowing where we are on the continuum and how much further we have to go, we can do certain things now to increase our earnings later on. We'll get to these in a minute.

First, let's talk about the value of lifetime earnings. In Chapter 3, I used the example of a 22-year-old who starts out earning $25,000 a year and receives annual raises of 5 percent a year over a 40-year career. By the time he retires, he will have received nearly $3 million in lifetime earnings. If he saves 10 percent of his salary each year and invests it at 8 percent, he will receive another million over the 40 years, for a total of $4 million. Sounds like a

lot of money, doesn't it? In fact, you could almost liken it to winning the lottery and having the money paid out in a series of installments (which often happens with large jackpots anyway).
What am I trying to say here? *You are your own lottery!* What's
more, *you* have control over how large the jackpot will be.

Let's bump up the stakes and see what your lifetime earnings would be if you started earning $50,000 at age 25 and re-
ceived raises of 10 percent a year. This situation would require
more education and training, as well as outstanding job performance throughout your career in order to merit such high
raises. The raises, by the way, don't have to come from the same
employer. In today's dynamic job market, strategic career moves
from one position to another and from one employer to another
enable ambitious people to get ahead of their more static counterparts. Over a lifetime our more aggressive career person would
receive a jackpot of (drum roll, please):

$$\$22,129,717$$

This is not some pie-in-the-sky number. It's what a 25-year-
old would earn over his or her working lifetime if a starting salary
were $50,000 and earnings increased by 10 percent a year. Need
I point out the odds of making $22 million this way versus buy-
ing a lottery ticket? Obviously, your own labor is the surest ticket
to wealth. All you have to do is be willing to work and be smart
about managing your career.

And what if you don't want to work 40 more years? Well,
you could stop after 20 years. By then you would have earned
a total of $2.8 million. Or work for 30 years and earn $8.2 million. Invest part of your salary along the way and you'll pick up
even more. No one says you have to kill yourself in order to become a multimillionaire, unless it's what you want. Regardless of
whether you go after the megabucks or have more modest career
aspirations, it's all within your control. Unlike the lottery, which
is hit or (mostly) miss, *you* can decide how much money you
want to make over your working lifetime. Is this a great country
or what?

And I'm not just saying this. As an investment executive, I work with some very successful people who have worked hard, made smart career choices, saved their money, and invested it wisely. Many are now reaping the rewards of their efforts. One client I'll call Lance, now at 68, looks back on a career that perfectly illustrates the kinds of strategic moves that can enable a person to get ahead and dramatically increase his or her earnings. Lance's first job out of college was as a buyer with an electronics company. He hated being chained to a desk, so as soon as he had an opportunity to become an outside salesperson he grabbed it (example of recognizing what makes you happy or unhappy on a job and doing something about it). Over the next two decades he excelled as a salesperson in the electronics industry, changing employers several times and taking classes to keep up with changes in the industry. In the 1980s he started his own electronics company. In the ensuing two decades the company has grown steadily and now employs 28 people and has more than $10 million in annual sales. Lance's two sons now run the business. Although Lance could easily afford to retire, he goes into the office 3 days a week because he says he likes being around young people. What's significant about Lance's story is that he did not have to make huge sacrifices to get where he is. He has always enjoyed his work and, even more important, has been able to achieve key financial goals for his family, such as living in a nice home and sending his three children to college.

THE VALUE OF EDUCATION

Bill Gates notwithstanding, a college degree can make a significant difference in the amount of money you earn over your lifetime. According to the Census Bureau, people with a bachelor's degree will earn, on average, nearly twice as much as people with only a high school diploma (up from one and a half times in 1975). Those with advanced degrees can expect to earn nearly three times as much as a typical high school graduate. And the gap keeps widening. Since 1990, the real (inflation-adjusted) median income of full-time workers has increased over 5 percent for those with a bachelor's degree and over 9 percent for those with advanced degrees, but has remained stagnant for high school graduates.

One of the best career moves you can make is to go to school. Do you have to go to Harvard or Princeton to make the big bucks? It doesn't hurt, but you certainly don't have to. In fact, *Fortune* magazine, in the May 1, 2000, story titled "Is Harvard Worth It?" (Jeremy Kahn, p. 201) addressed this very question. A study by Alan Krueger, an economist at Princeton, and Stacy Berg Dale, a researcher at the Andrew W. Mellon Foundation, found no economic advantage in attending a selective college. Their research looked at the earnings of the 1976 freshman class at 30 schools, ranging in selectivity (determined by average SAT scores) including Ivy League schools such as Yale, small private colleges, and large public universities. They concluded that smart, talented kids who attended less selective schools did just as well in their careers as their counterparts at elite colleges. There was no difference in average earnings. It seems the same traits that made the students desirable candidates for admission to Yale—ambition, intelligence, wit—carried over to the workplace, where they were duly rewarded even though they had turned down an elite education. In other words, it's the kid, not the college, that determines success.

And what about less formal education, such as certificate programs, seminars, online courses, workplace training sessions, and periodic classes featuring updated information relating to a specific industry? These all have value in helping workers either get ahead in their field or even switch to a new career. In many ways, these less formal but more practical (and less expensive!) avenues to knowledge can be of tremendous value, especially when you are being evaluated based on what you know, not where you went to school. Each industry differs. Computer programmers, for example, are hired and promoted based on the kind of programming they know how to do, and often these skills are learned on the job. Marketing people and other executives who engage in more strategic thinking may be evaluated based on where their degree is from, but they too need to keep up on the latest developments in their field.

One of the best things you can do to increase your jackpot of lifetime earnings is to get yourself educated and to keep learning throughout your career. Never has this been more true than in today's information age, where most companies consider knowledge and ideas their stock-in-trade.

THINKING LIKE AN ENTREPRENEUR

Whether your best career opportunities come through traditional jobs or a business you start yourself, you should always think of yourself as an entrepreneur and manage your career as if it were a business. You could even start using the terminology business owners use. Instead of earning a salary, you receive "revenues." Instead of working for an employer, you provide "services to customers" who pay you a fair price based on the going rate in the marketplace. You may have just one "customer" at a time, and it may seem that the "customer" sets the "purchase price" (your salary), but you can do a lot to influence that amount by selling the benefits of your services and showing how you can improve the "customer's" bottom line. And ultimately, you have control over which "customer" you choose to work with.

Don't ever worry about taking advantage of an employer by asking for a raise. If employees knew how much their companies were making off their skills and labors, they'd revolt. Microsoft, for example, receives about $28 billion in annual revenues and employs about 39,000 people. That works out to a little more than $700,000 in revenues per employee. Do you think salaries even approach this amount? Heck no. Bill Gates himself only collects $639,000 in salary. Of course, he makes it up in shares of stock. And to be fair, lots of Microsoft employees have gotten rich off Microsoft stock as well. But many companies today are making money off their employees' creativity and knowledge and, in my opinion, not sharing the booty to the extent they could. This may have been acceptable in the industrial age, when one employee's rivets were as good as another's, but when employees are providing the ideas that form the basis of a company's products, it seems employees ought to be duly rewarded.

GETTING PAID WHAT YOU'RE WORTH

One workplace custom employers have in their favor is that salary talk among employees is strictly taboo. Employees would rather spill the details of last night's date than reveal how much salary they earn. And no one would dare ask another employee what her salary is; that's worse than asking a woman how much she weighs. This, of course, gives employers the upper hand in setting salaries and in engaging in such unfair practices as offering a new hire more money than a loyal, longtime, hard-working employee receives for the same work. Employers justify it by saying they sometimes need to pay more to recruit a new hire, that it's the only way to attract top talent and stay competitive. This assumes, of course, that it's not necessary to pay existing talent top dollar and that existing employees don't know what top dollar is.

But now the Internet is starting to level the playing field. At www.salary.com you enter two pieces of information—the job title and city—and find out the average salary as well as the range of salaries for that job. There's a lot you can do with this information. First, if you are young and just starting to make career decisions, these salary levels can direct you toward the higher paying careers. Second, if you are considering a job change within your field or a move to a new geographic location, you can compare the different jobs against each other or the same job in different cities. Third, and most important, it can tell you if you're being paid what you're worth. If not, you have two main options available to you: Ask for a raise or update your resume and go job hunting.

If you like your present employer and want to stay (although I would have serious doubts about an employer who has been consistently underpaying me no matter how nice the people are), you'll want to develop a strategy for getting paid more. Although you could conceivably march into the boss's office, salary report in hand, and demand that you be paid what you're worth, a stealth approach may work better. This tactic involves defining your objective and making a series of subtle moves designed to get the boss to think it's his idea to pay you more. Of course, some bosses are denser than others so you may have to come right out and ask for a raise. But first, consider the following strategy.

1. Demonstrate your worth.

Doing a good job is only part of your function. Making sure everyone knows you're doing a good job reinforces your value to the company and justifies your salary. Keep in mind that employee salaries are generally considered expense items to a company. It is therefore in an employer's best interest to pay just enough to attract the talent it needs, but no more. But if you can point out the bottom-line benefits of your work—in other words, show the company how your being there nets the company more than it pays you in salary—you can be classified in your boss's mind as an investment, not an expense. By developing an entrepreneur's mindset, you should be able to think of ways to do this. Just imagine that you are a consultant or freelance _____ (whatever your job function is). When consultants sell their services, they must convince potential clients that hiring them will add to the bottom line in some way, either by reducing expenses or increasing revenues. To justify the expense of hiring the consultant, the savings or additional revenues must clearly be greater than the consultant's fee. Think about your job in the same way—understand your employer's business needs, work hard to earn your "fee," and take every opportunity to point out how you add value to the company. Keep a notebook of your accomplishments so you'll be prepared to talk specifics and you'll have an easier time updating your resume, if it comes to that.

2. Time your request.

After a few weeks or months of masterful selling in which you clearly demonstrate your value to the company, your boss will begin to realize that you're worth far more than you're currently being paid. This doesn't mean he or she will voluntarily offer you more money. After all, it's human nature to accept a bargain whenever we can get it. So it will be up to you to open negotiations to raise your "fee." The best time to do this is right after you've accomplished something important or achieved some notable success. At this time, your confidence level will be high, and your boss will be acutely aware of your work. If your company has a policy about doing salary reviews only at certain times of the year, you may be told to wait. But at least you will have made it clear that you expect more. If you are turned down flat or offered a lower raise than you think you deserve, ask your boss for a clear explanation and set a target date to review the situation again. Or pack your bags and go looking.

3. Ask for performance pay.

As an alternative to asking for a big salary increase, consider asking for a bonus instead. According to Hewitt Associates, salaries of executives were projected to rise by 4.4 percent in 2000, but one-time bonuses were expected to jump by 16 percent. That's because bonuses allow employers to link performance to profits, and companies would rather pay out a portion of their profits than assume an ongoing expense that permanently affects the bottom line. Once again, you are considering the business needs of the company and offering a solution that works for both you and your employer.

CHANGING JOBS

The time will come—and in this day and age it's likely to come sooner than later—when you will need to change jobs in order to improve your situation. As you learn more and become more accomplished in your work, you will want to keep moving into positions that allow you to develop your skills, offer greater value to your employer, and earn more money. Some of the larger, more progressive companies understand that the way to keep employees sharp and motivated is to offer opportunities for advancement. So it's conceivable that you could job hop within your own company and progress quite far in your career.

If your company is not like that, you'll need to periodically update your resume and put yourself on the market in order to move up in both status and pay. I can't overemphasize the importance of managing your career if you are truly interested in making a lot of money over your lifetime. It can be very easy to settle into an acceptable job and become complacent, especially if you like the people you work with and the pay is enough for you to get by. But that's not how you build wealth. The vast majority of lottery tickets are purchased by people in dead-end jobs because they see no other way out. But no one has to stay in a dead-end job. There are so many avenues to learning and so many jobs available that can start a person on a path to productivity that anyone who wants to make something of him- or herself can get on a career track that's both personally and financially rewarding. All it takes is motivation and the willingness to work.

Because there is so much career advice out there (a great site is www.careerjournal.com), and because every industry has its own set of customary practices, I will not attempt to offer specific ideas for job hunting, except to talk about some general attitudes you should maintain throughout your career. One is this idea of actively managing your career and constantly being on the lookout for ways to improve it by taking on challenging assignments that enable you to build your skills and periodically moving into positions that allow you to keep growing. Another is to find mentors who will take a personal interest in you and help you develop in your career. Experienced employees derive tremendous satisfaction from helping younger people excel, especially if they themselves were the product of mentoring. And finally, be sure to recognize the value of networking. Building and maintaining personal relationships is one age-old custom that has not been changed by the digital world. In fact, employers and employees alike are becoming disenchanted with the mega-job boards such as Monster.com and coming back to that tried-and-true practice that has always ensured a good fit: the personal referral. So be sure to nourish those relationships you establish along your career path; you never know when an old boss may end up working for you!

At some point you may benefit from career counseling or coaching. If you feel stuck in a job that no longer provides satisfaction and aren't sure where to go next, a career counselor can offer insight and direction. Career counseling today involves more than taking a few aptitude tests and learning how to write a resume. Today's counselors often call themselves coaches and cover the psychological and emotional aspects of work by asking questions such as "What gives you satisfaction?" and "What is it about your job that's keeping you from moving on?" Those specializing in coaching form a partnership with you and help you align your personal and professional lives through a process of discovery and clarification. Interview carefully, because the career counseling field is unregulated; anyone can hang out a shingle and call himself a coach or career counselor. For counseling referrals, check out the National Career Development Association (614-326-1750, www.ncda.org). For coaching referrals, go to the International Coach Federation (888-423-3131, www.coachfederation.org).

EVALUATING COMPENSATION PACKAGES

As you move up in your career, and especially as you consider job offers from new employers, be sure to look at the whole package, not just the annual salary. Employee benefits such as health insurance comprise a substantial portion of compensation packages today. And because health plans differ, you must consider these benefits from the standpoint of your own situation and not rely on rules of thumb. For example, if someone in your family depends on a prescription drug that costs $500 per month and if your new employer's health plan doesn't cover prescription drugs, you will now be out of pocket $6,000 a year. Better make sure the new job offers enough of a salary increase to offset that new cost. Also, if anyone in your family has a preexisting condition, you may need to wait a year before being covered by the new plan; if you have to pay the insurance premiums yourself that first year to keep your former insurance in force under the Consolidated Omnibus Budget Reconciliation Act (COBRA), you'll need to subtract that amount from your new salary to determine how much, if anything, you'll be ahead by switching jobs.

Another important benefit to consider when evaluating compensation packages is the company's 401(k) plan. Will the employer match part of your contribution? How soon can you start contributing? When do you become vested (that is, when does the employer's match become yours)? If your salary is $50,000, and if you contribute 10 percent or $5,000, and your employer matches half, that's another $2,500 added to your compensation over and above your salary. (Of course, the only way you can get it is by contributing the $5,000 and by staying with the company until you are vested. If that's not likely to be the case, don't count it.) When changing jobs, be sure to take the typical 1-year waiting period into account; if you have to forego the employer's match that first year, subtract it from your salary when doing your comparisons. Also consider any other retirement plans the company may be contributing to on your behalf. More about retirement plans in Chapter 5.

And finally, pay attention to a prospective employer's financial strength, an essential consideration if a significant part of your compensation package is stock options. The stock market being what it is, it's never possible to know in advance what stock options will turn out to be worth, but by doing some due diligence you can at least get an idea if they'll be worth something or zero. During the recent dot-com mania, many people left secure companies to go with startups offering many thousands of stock options, believing this would be their ticket to riches (and inspiring the writing of this book!). Many of those companies ran out of money before the much-anticipated initial public offering ever occurred, closing their doors and leaving people without a *job*, much less stock that was worth anything. Other startups went public as planned, but the stock promptly tanked in the marketplace, causing people's options to go underwater (i.e., become worthless).

You must consider two things when stock options are a part of your package: (1) the details of the plan, including how many options you'll be getting, the exercise price (the price at which you may purchase the stock), and the vesting schedule (when you become eligible to exercise the options); and (2) the anticipated future value of the stock. Since so many people are currently sitting on worthless options, I would recommend tackling the second of these considerations first. After all, if you're dealing with a company whose business model is so flawed that its stock is unlikely to ever be worth anything, there's no point in wasting your energy negotiating for another 10,000 options or a shorter vesting schedule. So before jumping in, size up the company as if you were making an investment in it, which you are. First, understand the company's basic business model: What are its products, who will buy them, and can the company make money doing this? Some business models that sounded good in the beginning turned out to be seriously flawed. For example, many of the failed dot-com companies based their financial projections on substantial online advertising revenues; when advertisers discovered that eyeballs didn't necessarily equate to sales, revenues plummeted and a lot of those companies went out of business. Also consider the experience of the management team. While an enthusiastic entrepreneur can be great at getting a round or two of venture capital funding and recruiting talented employees hoping to strike it rich, it takes someone with management experience to build a real company. Check out the education backgrounds and work experience of the management team; bios are often posted on the Web.

Only after you are convinced of the company's financial viability should you get serious about taking the position. This is not to say you should never go with a startup, especially if you're young and have little to lose. There's no denying that many people have made millions betting on untested ideas that worked out. But the environment is different now, and investors are demanding more than just a good idea and the promise of profitability in, oh, a few years or so. If you are considering going with a company that has no profits at present, at least understand how and when those profits are due to materialize, and do a gut check to make sure it all makes sense to you. Only then should you get into the nitty-gritty negotiations concerning exercise price and vesting schedules. Stock options can be complicated, so study up. You'll find lots of useful information at www.mystockoptions.com. You may also want to get advice from someone who specializes in such matters.

One last word on stock options: Don't let them derail a fast-moving career. In the aftermath of the dot-com mania, many employees are now stuck in jobs they hate with companies they've become disillusioned with because their options haven't vested yet. (Let this be a lesson to anyone negotiating an options package to secure as short a vesting schedule as possible.) It may be a sign that it's time to cut and run if you're feeling stuck and if your options aren't (and may never be) worth anything. Why waste valuable time in a place that's doing nothing for your career? Consider the time you spent a valuable learning experience and move on.

STARTING YOUR OWN BUSINESS

Many of my wealthy clients got that way by owning their own businesses. You don't have to aspire to billionairedom when considering entrepreneurship. You can start a small company and build it into a thriving concern with several million dollars in sales, as my client Lance did, and make a very nice life for yourself. Or, you can enter one of the professions, such as law or medicine, and build a successful practice, either working as a sole practitioner or in a group with other professionals. Entrepreneurship does not require a unique idea that nobody's ever thought of before (in fact, those kinds of businesses are at greater risk of failure because no market has been established). All you have to do is identify a need and figure out a way to meet it. For ideas, just look around you and see what's missing.

Of course, not all of the needs in the marketplace will coincide with your own skills and interests. The key is to integrate what the market needs with what you have to offer. One without the other is no good. So if you start by identifying the need, you must then see if you are in a position to fill it, considering your education, experience, talents, interests, and ability to round up all the necessary outside resources to complete your offering. Conversely, if your education and experience point you to a specific type of business, as Lance's did in the electronics industry, you must determine if there is a need for what you have to offer and if that need will still be around for the foreseeable future. This is why career planning is so important. As you move along your career path building education and experience, you want to do it in a field that has legs, so to speak, otherwise your business won't last. This advice goes for anyone planning a long-term career, not just entrepreneurs.

Entrepreneurship seldom happens overnight. Usually, people think about it for awhile and start laying groundwork before all the pieces fall into place. Try to do as much of this as you can while you're still working for an employer and have a steady salary coming in. Things you can do in your off hours include researching possible businesses to start, compiling information about other businesses in the field, learning more about your market and the best way to reach customers, and planning the details of the operations such as locating suppliers. I can't emphasize enough the importance of planning before making your big move. Once you remove that employer-sponsored safety net that includes a steady salary, health insurance, retirement plan benefits, vacations and sick days, free photocopying, and all the pens your conscience will allow you to steal, you are on your own. Forewarned is forearmed.

Unless you buy a going concern, a brand-new business, in the beginning, will have no money coming in. One of the reasons new businesses fail is that the entrepreneur didn't realize how hard it would be to generate ongoing revenues. Initial financing can go only so far. Pretty soon your friends and family (the most common source of funding for new businesses) will want to see a return on their investment; and even if they don't, it's amazingly easy to burn through the initial stake of cash. If the business can't sustain itself by then, your next source of funds may be angel financing. Angels are like friends and family except you don't know them yet; they are private investors who are willing to take a chance on a new business, however they definitely do expect a return on their investment. This means you'd better have a well-thought-out business plan and an ironclad formula for making money. Many entrepreneurs today finance their new businesses with credit cards. I won't say this is a terrible idea, because many businesses have gotten off the ground this way. Just be sure to factor the interest costs into your financial projections and understand that if the business doesn't get up and running fast, you could be stuck with a lot of personal debt. I would also caution against draining your 401(k) plan to start a business because it's awfully hard to recoup those savings. Even if your business succeeds, you're going to need money for retirement, so why not keep at least one safe harbor to balance all the risk taking you plan to do?

THE IMPORTANCE OF BALANCE

I promise not to deliver a lecture on slowing down when your passion right now is making a lot of money. As long as you're not neglecting the people who are important to you, the focused pursuit of wealth can be a worthwhile activity and far preferable to lazing on a beach somewhere, piña colada in hand (that part comes later). But do understand the concept of burnout. When burnout occurs, usually through overwork and lack of balance, your motivation comes to a screeching halt and you become completely ineffective. You hate what you're doing and find it nearly impossible to go on. You become a walking zombie. And the worst part is you don't know how to get yourself out. You feel stuck, trapped, and horrible. Don't let this happen to you. Keep enough balance in your life that you don't get burned out on what you're doing. If you start feeling the initial signs of burnout—malaise, a vague dissatisfaction with your job or your life—do not sweep them under the rug. They'll only fester and get worse. Those initial signs of burnout are telling you that you need to make a change. Do it before it's too late.

I hope this chapter has given you a better sense of how valuable your own talents and labors can be in building wealth over your lifetime. Between the amount you earn, the amount you save, and the wisdom with which you invest, you have all the ingredients of your own personal fortune.

CHAPTER FIVE

THE SURE AND STEADY ROAD TO RICHES

Long-range planning does not deal with future decisions, but with the future of present decisions.

Peter F. Drucker

Ask thy purse what thou should spend.

Scottish proverb

A SURVEY BY THE CONSUMER FEDERATION OF AMERICA showed that one-quarter of Americans really do think their best chance to build wealth for retirement is by playing the lottery, not by patiently saving and investing. I'm sure you're not one of those, but since everyone has contemplated winning the lottery at one time or another, consider the following facts:

- If you buy a lottery ticket, your odds of winning a $3 million lottery jackpot are about one in 23 million.
- If you start a savings plan now, your odds of compiling $3 million during your lifetime are much better than one in 23 million—maybe even 100 percent, depending on when you start and how much you are able to save.
- If you don't start a savings plan and you keep buying lottery tickets every week and you don't win the lottery or receive other type of windfall, your odds of ever having $3 million are zero. Plus, you are out the cost of the lottery tickets.

Most people approach saving all wrong. They calculate their budget, including fixed and variable expenses such as rent, car payments, insurance, food, and others, and then see if there's any money left over for saving. Usually there's not. So a better way to approach it is to first commit to saving a certain amount based on your goals (from Chapter 3) or, if you don't want to get that specific, decide to save a percentage of your income, say 5 or 10 percent. After that's taken off the top, you can calculate your budget based on what's left. Now, this practice may require some lifestyle changes. If you've already committed to an apartment, a car payment, and other expenses that keep you living just within your means, you need to figure out how to free up the required savings—not an impossibility. Look around you: Lots of people make less money than you yet they seem to manage okay. You probably made less money a few years ago than you do now, but lifestyle creep (which all successful people are subject to) has made it so there's never any money left over at the end of the month. What's called for is a different approach.

When I emphasize the importance of saving, I'm doing it for you, so you can have the things you want in life. Dinner out tonight or a vacation this summer? A high-rent apartment now or retire two years earlier? These are the kinds of choices you are faced with in life. Spend now, or save the money so you can spend more later? You decide.

ARE YOU A PROSPERITY THINKER OR A SCARCITY THINKER?

Prosperity thinkers believe there is a limitless supply of money in the universe. They believe that if you want to spend more, all you have to do is make more. Scarcity thinkers, conversely, believe there is a finite supply of money and if you want to spend more here, you must cut back there. Nearly everyone falls into one of these two groups, and which one generally dictates their money-earning and money-saving activities throughout their lifetimes. Prosperity thinkers tend to own their own businesses and see a limitless supply of customers and revenues. They are often aggressive investors and don't mind losing money because they assume it will be easy to make it back. When faced with the choice of spending less or earning more, they would definitely choose to earn more. Scarcity thinkers tend to have jobs with fixed salaries, and the idea of finding ways to bring more money into their lives simply doesn't occur to them. They are very conservative investors and have a hard time dealing with risk of any kind. When faced with the choice of spending less or earning more, they would always choose to spend less.

There are many marriages in which one spouse is a prosperity thinker and the other is a scarcity thinker. This dichotomy can either create an ideal balance or cause big fights over money. The prosperity thinker doesn't want to cut back on the budget (or even deal with the budget) because he or she truly believes everything will all work out. Saving really isn't necessary because there will always be plenty of money coming in. The scarcity thinker becomes crazed by this. "Don't you see," he or she exclaims, "you're spending too much! We've got to get a handle on our finances! If we don't start saving now we'll never be able to retire (or send the kids to college, or whatever)!"

The ideal place to be is somewhere in between the two extremes. By believing there's plenty of money out there, prosperity thinkers seem to be able to attract more of it into their lives. Scarcity thinkers don't, and their belief that the supply of money is limited probably has something to do with it. Prosperity thinkers can be unrealistic at times, going on spending sprees and living on the edge because their beliefs about how easy it is to attract money are inflated and exaggerated. While they may have periods of exceptionally high income, they can also hit the wall. And because they seldom do any long-term planning, they may find themselves unprepared for major goals such as retirement. Scarcity thinkers may set their sights lower and may not ever earn as much as the prosperity thinkers, but they are far more likely to meet their goals, modest though they may be.

If you are investing as a couple and have fights about money because of your differing orientations, I urge each of you to recognize your differences and work toward understanding—and learning from—the other. If you're a scarcity thinker, understand that by changing your attitude, money may begin to flow more easily into your life. If you're a prosperity thinker, try to exercise some caution in your financial dealings—for your spouse's sake if not your own. If you are single and lean heavily toward one orientation or the other, try to achieve a balance between the two by telling yourself things like, "I know it's easy to make money but I still have to plan," or "I'm tired of living like a pauper; it's time to figure out how to bring in more money."

STARTING A SAVINGS PLAN

If you are not currently saving, or if you feel you are not saving enough, your first assignment is to commit to saving a certain amount every month. Start by writing your monthly take-home pay on a blank piece of paper. Underneath that write down the amount you want to save every month. Do not consider your monthly budget when determining your savings amount; that's doing it backwards, remember? Instead, consider the goals you wrote down from the worksheet that is Figure 3-1. If you are contributing to a 401(k) plan, your take-home pay already reflects some savings; if you feel this is enough to fund your retirement then you do not need to include retirement savings in this exercise. You will, however, need to include savings for items such as college, vacations, new car, your emergency fund, and any other items you identified from Figure 3-1.

Here's an example:

Monthly take-home pay	$4,000
Desired monthly savings	– 400
Amount available for living expenses	$3,600

Find Out Where Your Money Goes

Now it's time to see if you can actually live on the amount available after you've taken your savings off the top. Ready for a fun exercise? Pull out your bank statements or checking account registers and credit card statements for the past year and lay them out on the table. For each month, add up all your deposits and write down the total. Then add up all your expenditures (checks, cash withdrawals, credit card charges, and monthly interest charges if you don't pay your credit card balance in full) and write down the total. Now compare your expenditures to your deposits. This is likely to be a very enlightening experience. In some months your expenditures may have exceeded your income. If you are one of the many people who do not pay their credit card bills in full every month, look at your balance from one month to the next. Is it getting bigger? This is a real danger sign and shows that you need to get your spending under control before you can embark on the serious pursuit of wealth.

Next, review each expenditure and put it into one of three categories: "had to spend," "didn't have to spend," and "not sure." Items such as rent or mortgage payments, utilities, car payments, child care, and insurance premiums obviously fall into the "had to spend" category. (You may not have needed to spend *this much* on these essential items, but in most cases you can't immediately cut them out of your budget. More on this shortly.) Things like dinners out, concerts, anything purchased at the mall that you didn't really need (clothes, CDs, books, tools, cosmetics, etc.) would go into the "didn't have to spend category." "*Wait a minute*," I can hear you say. "I *need* cosmetics (tools)." Fine, then, put them into the "had to spend" category. But you must admit that the third lipstick or the specialty tool that you've heretofore lived quite nicely without would have to fall into the "didn't have to spend" category. Such decisions are unquestionably the hardest part of the exercise, but it's very important to get a handle on your "had to spend" and "didn't have to spend" categories, because going forward you will be making this distinction *before* you spend the money. Any items you're not sure about—cash withdrawals or expenditures you can't remember—would go into the "not sure" category.

If you have a lot of expenditures in the "not sure" category—and this can happen if you pay cash for a lot of things or you do much of your shopping at big discount stores where you're writing one check for everything from groceries to the gadget *du jour*—you get to do another exercise. First, think about your spending habits and try to estimate what percentage of your cash is spent on "had to spend" versus "didn't have to spend" items. For example, if you hit up the ATM for $50 a week and spend it all on lunches and parking, it would all fall into the "had to spend" category. If you spend about $25 on lunches and don't know where the rest of it goes, it's likely the other $25 would go into the "didn't have to spend" category. (That amounts to $1,300 in a year—see how easy it is to free up extra money for saving?) Do the same with the discount store expenditures: allocate, say 80 percent to "had to spend" and 20 percent to "didn't have to spend" categories depending on your usual shopping habits.

If you feel comfortable with this ballpark method of allocation and believe it represents your true spending, you can escape the next part of the exercise, which is for people who really want to get a handle on where their money goes. For the next 3 or 6 or 12 months, keep a record of every dime you spend by writing it down in a notebook you carry with you at all times. In the notebook make five columns: date, item purchased, amount spent, "had to spend" and "didn't have to spend." In the last two columns you'll make a checkmark to indicate which category the expenditure falls into. Of course, you may not have very many in the "didn't have to spend" category because the exercise itself may discourage you from spending money on things you don't need. That's not necessarily the point here. This exercise is not designed to deprive you of things that will make your life happier, it's only meant to help you get a grasp on your spending so you can make decisions about whether to spend now or save it for later.

It's very important not to place judgment on yourself or your spouse when doing this exercise. Everyone gets sloppy in their spending at times. What matters is that you are turning over a new leaf and vowing not to go back to your old ways. In fact, the more frivolous expenditures you can identify, the more successful your new savings plan will be because you won't have to make major changes to your lifestyle; all you have to do is reallocate a portion of your "didn't have to spend" budget to savings. And remember, this is all about choice. The reason you're saving instead of making those impulse purchases that the retailers and advertisers of the world try so hard to make you want is so you can have the things you really want in life.

Once you've classified each expenditure into its category for each of the preceding 12 months, add up all the "had to spend" amounts and divide by 12 to get the monthly average. Is it less than the "Amount available for living expenses" you identified at the beginning of this exercise ($3,600 in the example)? If so you're in great shape to meet your savings goals. Now that you know you won't go hungry, you can commit to taking your savings amount off the top, knowing you're only cutting into the "didn't have to spend" part of the budget. Then it just becomes a matter of spending less on those discretionary items, which will be easy to do if you've already put your savings amount into a mutual fund so it's not available for spending.

When Money Is Really Tight

If your "had to spend" items exceed the "Amount available for living expenses," then you have some important decisions to make. One, you can scale back your goals and reduce your savings requirement. Two, you can make some major lifestyle changes in order to reduce your "had to spend" items. Or three, you can do a combination of the two. Again, it comes down to a choice between spending now or spending later. So first take a look at your goals. Are you being overly ambitious in your goals, wanting fancy vacations and Harvard for the kids? These goals may require too great a sacrifice now. If money is tight, it might be better to scale back your goals so you can reduce your savings requirement. However, if your goals are relatively modest and do not lend themselves to cutting back, then you may need to make some lifestyle changes so you can meet your saving goals. These lifestyle changes would be designed either to cut your expenses or bring in more money or a combination of both.

You may see these changes as pretty drastic, but if they put you on more solid financial footing, you'll feel better about doing them. With each, you'll need to weigh the costs of making the change against the amount you'll save. For example, if your rent is high you may consider moving to a cheaper apartment. But if the move would put you so far away from your job that you'd burn up any rent savings in commuting costs, then obviously it's not worth it. Look at all of your essential expenses and consider how a lifestyle change could reduce them: Could you save car expenses by taking public transportation or trading in your newer model car (and monthly car payments) for an older model? Could you save child care expenses by working a different shift so one parent is always home? Should you ask for a raise or look for a new job that pays more? Could you get a second job working a few evenings a week or one day on the weekend? Get your creative juices flowing and you'll be surprised by how many solutions you come up with. Not all will be acceptable to you, but by brainstorming a bit you can throw all the possible solutions out onto the table and then explore each one in more detail.

If you've never had a savings plan before, I can't tell you how good it feels to know that every month you are setting aside funds for the future. At first it may feel like a sacrifice. But once you see the funds build up, you'll be convinced you're doing the right thing. Just imagine: Every month you can take, say, $400 worth of "didn't need to spend" money, put it into a mutual fund that averages 8 percent returns, and have nearly $30,000 in 5 years, or $73,000 in 10 years. If you increase your savings by 10 percent every year, your savings will turn into $37,000 in 5 years or $116,000 in 10 years. If you earn more than 8 percent, you'll accumulate even more (however, for planning purposes count on 8 percent; it's better to be pleasantly surprised if you earn more than your assumptions than to be disappointed if you don't). Then when the time comes to spend that money on something you've been wanting, or to be in a position to retire early, you'll be so glad you got a handle on your finances when you did.

EASY WAYS TO SAVE

You know how the federal government makes employers withhold part of employee salaries for taxes? The Internal Revenue Service is no dummy. It knows that if people ever got their hands on that money it would have a heck of a time collecting taxes. Same with Social Security taxes. Very simply, what you don't see you can't spend. You know this. So one of the most effective things you can do to save money is to have it put into savings before you even see it. This does not mean you are weak. Well, maybe it does, but everyone is. It's human nature to spend money if it's available. The trick is to make it unavailable, or at least make it so hard to get to that we are forced to ask ourselves:

"Do I really need this thing that I'm about to foolishly spend my hard-earned money on?" That moment of reflection may be all it takes to bring us to our senses and make us realize that the long-term goals we are saving for are more important than today's impulse purchase. If you really want the item that's threatening to convert you from a careful saver to a shameful spender, add it to your goal list and treat it as you would any other goal. Chances are, other goals on your list would take priority.

401(k) Plans

If you work for a company that offers a 401(k) plan, there's a good chance you are already participating. Eighty percent of all eligible workers do, and if companies start making enrollment automatic (meaning you would have to opt out if you didn't want to participate), even more people will get into the retirement savings habit. This practice is extremely important because, as you may have observed, the responsibility for preparing for retirement is now falling squarely on our shoulders. Our fathers and grandfathers very likely worked for corporations that contributed to a retirement plan on their behalf, enabling them to retire with a lifetime pension that they didn't have to save for. Today, most companies have replaced that type of pension with the 401(k) plan, which requires you to make conscious decisions about whether to participate, how much to save, and where to invest the money. This policy is really in the best interests of everyone, because it gives you more control over your retirement benefits. Even more important, it gives you career flexibility. No longer must you stay with one company to age 65 in order to receive your share of retirement benefits. You can move from job to job and take your retirement savings with you (more on this in the next section).

BENEFITS OF 401(K) PLANS

For four reasons 401(k) plans are ideal savings plans: (1) They deduct the money before you get it. (2) The amount you save is deducted from your taxable income for the year. (3) You can invest your savings any way you want (using the options offered by your plan) and the investment earnings build up free from current taxes. (4) Your employer may match part of your savings. Let's look at each of these in more detail.

Automatic Savings

The great thing about having a set amount withheld from your paycheck every month is that it's very hard (if not impossible) to override the system. This means two things: (1) You are forced to save a fixed amount every month, even when you're feeling poor; and (2) you achieve what's called *time diversification* when investing in stocks. Investing is discussed in more detail in the following chapters, but basically the automatic savings plan saves you from having to decide when is the best time to enter the market. Imagine if you had a large lump sum available to invest right now. Would you want to put it all into the market now, or would it be better to wait 6 months or a year? With your automatic savings program you are spared this decision because you are not faced with investing a huge amount at one time. Because you're investing little by little, it's always the right time to invest in the market. If stock prices go lower from here, that's fine because next time you'll get more shares for your money. If they go higher that's fine too, because it means your money is growing. You may have heard the term *dollar cost averaging*. Same idea. When prices are lower you get more shares for the same amount of money, which lowers your average cost per share.

Tax Deduction

Actually, with a 401(k) plan what you get is better than a tax deduction because you don't even have to worry about finding the little box on the tax form that enables you to take the deduction. In legal parlance, 401(k) plans are called "salary reduction plans." Why anybody ever thought an employee would sign up for a plan with a name like that is beyond me. What it really means is that your salary is reduced for tax purposes. If you earn $50,000 and contribute $5,000 to the 401(k) plan, your income will be reported as $45,000. If you are in the 28 percent federal tax bracket, that saves you an immediate $1,350. You get this by either adjusting your withholding so your take-home pay is about $112 more every month or receiving a tax refund when you file your taxes. (It's better to adjust your withholding so you're not giving the government an interest-free loan; to maximize your savings, take the extra $112 and put it into a mutual fund instead.)

Tax-Deferred Earnings

Investment earnings within a 401(k) account (and several other types of accounts which are discussed later in this chapter) build up free from current taxes. To better illustrate this concept, let's look at the flip side: investing in a taxable account. New investors often don't understand that investment earnings are normally taxable, so they would naturally have a hard time appreciating the benefit of a tax-deferred retirement account. But if you are a successful investor outside of your retirement account, Uncle Sam will want part of your earnings. If your savings account earns $500 in interest this year, you must report this amount on your tax return and, if you are in the 27 percent federal tax bracket, pay $135 in taxes, effectively reducing your $500 to $365. This may not sound like a lot of money, but when your investment account grows larger over the years, through your own savings and compounded investment returns, it can make a big difference. For example, let's say you're getting close to retirement and your nest egg has grown to $800,000. With an 8 percent return, one year's investment earnings would be $64,000. If you're in the 27 percent tax bracket (actually, this could push you into a higher bracket), you would pay $17,280 in taxes, effectively reducing your investment earnings to $46,720. Instead of earning 8 percent on your money, you're earning 5.84 percent. Uncle Sam earns the other 2.16 percent. Once you know how severe the tax bite can be (more on this in Chapter 9), you will make every effort to shield your investment earnings from taxes. And you will appreciate how much of a gift your company's 401(k) plan is for allowing you to earn all the investment returns you want and not pay a penny in taxes. Of course, when you eventually take the money out of the account you will need to report it on your tax return. But by then you may be in a lower bracket. At the very least you can control how much you take out and when, so you can minimize the tax burden.

Employer Match

More than 80 percent of employers offering 401(k) plans match part of their employees' contributions. According to a recent study, 37 percent matched 50 cents on the dollar, while 25 percent matched dollar for dollar. The rest matched varying amounts; some even matched more than dollar for dollar. Needless to say, these contributions are like free money and should serve as a very strong incentive for people to contribute as much as possible to their 401(k) plan and to stay with the company until the employer's portion becomes vested (usually 3 to 7 years; read your plan documents to find out).

MANAGING YOUR CAREER AND YOUR 401(K) PLAN

It's clear that 401(k) plans have caught on with corporate America and with employees who voluntarily sign up because they understand the powerful tax and savings benefits. But what hasn't caught on yet is the importance of managing your 401(k) plan throughout your working career. The biggest mistake people make is failing to preserve their account balance when they change jobs. A recent study by Hewitt Associates found that 57 percent of participants cashed out their 401(k) plans when they changed jobs. This meant they had to pay income taxes on the money and, in most cases, a 10 percent early withdrawal penalty as well. Someone in a combined state and federal tax bracket of 35 percent who's under age 59 1/2 would pay nearly half their account balance to the government. And more than likely they spent what was left over. Without even thinking about it, they totally decimated their retirement seed money, denying themselves the chance to build it into a much bigger nest egg. Let's take the example of someone who leaves a company with $10,000 in their

401(k) plan and chooses to take the cash. After paying $4,500 in taxes and penalties they have $5,500 left. If they spend it on a down payment on a car (which starts depreciating in value the moment it's driven off the lot), they have zero left. If they take the $5,500 and invest it in a taxable account earning 8 percent (5.84 percent after tax), they'll have $30,190 in 30 years. But if they take the whole $10,000 and put it into an IRA rollover account earning 8 percent tax deferred, they'll have $100,626 in 30 years. And that's without adding another penny to it. By simply ignoring the money, they can build it into a substantial sum.

So an extremely important part of building wealth is to actively manage your retirement plan throughout your working career—to take advantage of its portability to move from job to job (always paying attention to vesting schedules so as not to lose the employer match) and to preserve its tax-favored status as you move around. There are three ways to do this:

1. If it's more than $5,000, you can leave it where it is at your old company. However, many people feel they might miss out on updated communications so they often choose one of the other two options.
2. Transfer the balance to your new employer's 401(k) plan. However, some companies require you to be with the company a year before joining the 401(k) plan. In this case you would probably choose the third option, at least during the waiting period.
3. Have your account balance transferred to an IRA rollover account. This option is becoming very popular, especially for frequent job changers. After you leave each job, you dump your 401(k) plan assets into your IRA rollover account, which becomes larger and larger as you move toward retirement. Rather than being limited to the investment options offered by the various employers, you can invest the money any way you want and be personally responsible for managing it. Then when you retire and dump your last 401(k) account balance into it, it becomes your primary source of retirement income. You withdraw

funds as needed and continue to manage the rest of it so it will grow throughout your retirement. Although you can open an IRA rollover account with almost any mutual fund, having your account at a brokerage firm offers more investing options, including the ability to choose from hundreds of mutual fund families as well as investing in individual stocks and bonds.

COMPARING 401(K) PLANS

Another important aspect of managing your career and your 401(k) plan is to be savvy about what constitutes a good 401(k) plan and to become an expert in comparing the various plans as you evaluate job opportunities throughout your working career. Obviously, a company that doesn't offer a 401(k) plan at all would not be equal to one that does offer such a plan. A company without a plan would have to offer far more in salary and other benefits in order to make its total compensation package equivalent to that of a company with a good 401(k) plan. When comparing 401(k) plans, consider the following:

Evaluate the Employer Match

This item relates to hard dollars, so it's one of the most important aspects of a plan. However, if you receive an offer of a higher salary from a company with a lower match, you'll have to do the math to compare the two offers.

Check the Vesting Schedule

A generous employer match only has value if you stay with the company long enough to claim it. (Your own contributions and the earnings on both your and your employer's contributions vest immediately.) Look at the plan's vesting schedule to see when the match money becomes yours. Keep this vesting schedule in mind as you make your career decisions. If a great job opportunity comes along before you're vested, you'll have to weigh the tradeoff between leaving money on the table versus taking the better offer.

Consider the Investment Options

Companies may offer anywhere from three to dozens of investment options, which are usually mutual funds or annuities. They range from a simple stock/bond/money market selection to a whole array of investment choices including international funds, small stock funds, sector funds (such as technology), and several kinds of bond funds. Obviously, the more choices there are, the more investment flexibility you have. When you leave a company and face the choice between rolling your 401(k) money into your new employer's plan or to an IRA rollover account, consider the investment options in the new plan; if they're limited, go with the IRA rollover.

Look at Costs

There are two kinds of costs: administrative fees and mutual fund expense ratios. Many employers bear the costs of administration, so employees usually don't need to worry about that part. Expense ratios are charged by the mutual funds for their services in managing the money. While it's worth paying attention to these fees, a 401(k) plan's fees are not likely to be the determining factor in choosing one company over another based on the total compensation package. Still, it pays to be alert to ongoing fees because they can cut into your investment returns over time. If you think your plan's fees are too high, talk to management about reviewing the plan's investment options.

Consider the Investment Education Provided

How good is the company at communicating the plan and educating you on investments? For many people, the 401(k) plan is their first venture into saving and investing. Until now, money has always been something to spend, so when faced with terms like "asset allocation," "large cap stocks," and "high-yield bonds," they have no idea what those terms mean. It's nice to have a choice in investing, but not if you have no clue what you're doing. Investment education should be a key component of your 401(k) plan. If it's not, you'll need to educate yourself, by reading books like this and perhaps taking courses on investing and personal finance.

Other Tax-Deferred Retirement Plans

If you work for a company that does not offer a 401(k) plan, or if you are self-employed, you have to find other ways to save for retirement. Unlike your 401(k) counterpart who merely needs to check a few boxes on a form to start a lifelong habit of saving for retirement, you need to actively seek out opportunities to save. Nothing else quite matches the 401(k) plan for its ease of saving (automatic withholding) and employer match (free money). However, you can get some pretty good tax benefits with other types of plans, and you can always set up an automatic savings program through a mutual fund or brokerage account. Some or all of the following may be available to you, even if you also contribute to a 401(k) plan and want to save even more. If you do not contribute to a 401(k) plan, they may be your only chance to build a retirement fund, and you will need to proactively open and contribute to them; no one will do it for you.

QUALIFIED RETIREMENT PLANS FOR BUSINESS OWNERS AND SELF-EMPLOYED INDIVIDUALS

If you own a small business or are self-employed, you can contribute to your own retirement plan. Retirement plans for businesses can be very simple or very complex, depending on the type of business you have, whether you have employees, and what your goals are. The discussion here is limited to the most common plans for self-employed people without employees because the others are just too complex and require customized advice that takes into account a myriad of factors.

Whether your business is your main occupation or you run a small side business in addition to your regular job, contact a brokerage firm about setting up your own retirement plan. The brokerage firm will provide the necessary paperwork and instructions. Once you've funded the plan by depositing your check sometime before your tax filing deadline, you can invest the funds any way you want, depending on the products and services offered by the firm you select.

Profit-Sharing or Keogh Plan

With this type of plan you can contribute up to $40,000 in 2002. Your contribution is tax deductible, which means you must find the little box on the tax form and enter the correct amount. By making the contribution and finding the little box, you can reduce your taxable income by the amount of your contribution and save hard tax dollars. For example, if you contribute $12,000 to your retirement plan and you are in the 30 percent federal tax bracket, your tax bill will be reduced by $3,600 ($12,000 × 0.30). This means you are out of pocket not $12,000, but $8,400 ($12,000 − $3,600). Yet the whole $12,000 belongs to you and stays in your account to grow. This tax deduction makes profit-sharing (Keogh) plans nearly as good as 401(k) plans; what you lack in employer match you make up in the ability to contribute a higher amount. And, as with all retirement plans, your investment earnings grow tax deferred. The deadline to establish a Keogh plan is December 31, but you do not have to fund it until you file your tax return.

SEP-IRA (Simplified Employee Pension Individual Retirement Account)

A SEP-IRA is similar to a Keogh plan but is somewhat easier to administer. Also, if you miss the December 31 deadline, you can open a SEP-IRA as late as your tax filing deadline.

TRADITIONAL IRA

If your company does not offer a retirement plan of any kind, you may wish to contribute to a traditional IRA. Or, if your company does offer a retirement plan but your adjusted gross income (AGI) is less than $33,000 if single or $53,000 if married filing jointly in 2001 (and rising by $1,000 per year in future years), you may wish to take advantage of this rather pitiful way to save. I say pitiful because although Congress just raised the contribution limit, it still won't get you to retirement on its own. The new contribution limits are as follows: $3,000 for years 2002–2004; $4,000 for years 2005–2007; and $5,000 for 2008. After 2008, the contribution limit will be indexed for inflation in $500 increments. Also, there is now a new catch-up provision for people 50 and over. If you're late getting started saving, you can contribute an additional $500 in years 2002 through 2005, and $1000 in 2006 and thereafter. Although the amounts are meager for anyone who is serious about saving for retirement, IRAs are still valuable savings vehicles due to the tax-deferred buildup, so be sure to contribute if you are eligible to take the tax deduction (i.e., no retirement plan at work or income less than the amounts just noted). But don't let it be your only retirement savings plan.

ROTH IRA

Here's an account that nearly everyone who is not eligible for the traditional IRA tax deduction should take advantage of because the investment earnings build up not just tax deferred, but tax free. The contribution limit is as pitiful as it is for traditional IRAs, but unlike traditional IRAs and all other types of retirement savings plans, when you take withdrawals from a Roth IRA the income is completely tax free. This is a tremendous boon, especially if your Roth IRA grows to a large amount (through annual contributions and converted IRA rollovers) and becomes your main source of retirement income. You do not get a tax deduction in the year you make your contribution, but the tax advantages at the other end can be significant. There's just one catch. You can't contribute to a Roth IRA if your adjusted gross income is over $110,000 if single or $160,000 if married filing jointly. (If it's over $95,000 if single or $150,000 if married filing jointly you can make a partial contribution.) The Roth IRA has several other features that make it a great retirement and estate planning vehicle, but for now, just open one (if you're eligible) and make your contributions every year, even if you also contribute to a 401(k) or other type of retirement plan. By the way, your *total* IRA contribution is limited to the amounts previously noted ($2,000 in 2001, $3,000 in 2002–2004, and so on). For example, you can't contribute $2,000 to a traditional IRA and $2,000 to a Roth IRA. If you are eligible for the tax deduction on a traditional IRA (i.e., no retirement plan at work or income less than the stated amounts), go with the traditional IRA, otherwise go with the Roth.

Tax-Deferred Saving for College

This chapter explains some of the more popular tax-favored savings plans because that's where you should start your saving. Before putting part of your after-tax salary into a taxable account, it's usually better to use up all of the tax-favored plans available to you first. The only reason you might not want to do this is if you are saving for near-term goals. Most tax-deferred plans have a catch of some kind—age restrictions on taking money out of retirement plans, for example—and you don't want to incur penalties if you don't have to. However, the tax benefits are pretty hard to beat and in some cases it makes sense to contribute even if you know you'll be taking some of the money out early.

The Section 529 plan is a tax-favored savings plan designed to help parents and grandparents save for college. There are several other tax-advantaged programs available for college, such as the Education IRA, but it only allows you to save $2,000 per year beginning in 2002 (up from $500 in 2001). The Section 529 plan allows you to stash up to $10,000 per year away for college (in some cases, more) and have the earnings grow tax free. These plans are sometimes confused with prepaid tuition plans, from which they evolved, but they are very different and vastly more flexible. With a prepaid tuition plan, you would essentially choose the college your child would attend and pay the tuition in advance to protect against inflation driving up the cost. These plans weren't very popular because who could tell if their 3-year-old would want to attend college at all, much less the selected college? And, of course, investment returns were limited to the extent of the increase in college costs.

Section 529 plans are designed to enable parents to save for any college, for any child, and to earn investment returns exceeding the rate of inflation if they are willing to take the risk. If Susie ends up not going to college, the funds can be used for another family member, even the parents themselves. The only requirement is that the funds be used for "qualified" educational expenses such as tuition, books, and room and board at any accredited postsecondary educational institution, undergraduate or graduate. If the money is used for something else, you have to pay a 10 percent penalty in addition to the tax. This applies to the earnings only; your own contributions are not subject to either tax or penalty.

Although there is a federal law providing for such plans, the 529 programs are sponsored by the states, which have the freedom to structure the plans differently with respect to the maximum amount you can contribute, the flexibility to change beneficiaries, and how the funds can be invested, among other terms. You don't have to use the plan sponsored by the state you live in. In fact, choosing the right vehicle for your 529 savings is a key part of the strategy. For example, one of the mutual fund companies I work with has developed a 529 investment program that utilizes Rhode Island's plan. After scrutinizing all of the states' 529 plans, this mutual fund found that Rhode Island's plan offered the highest contribution limits and maximum flexibility with regard to investments and beneficiary changes as compared to other states' plans.

The 529 plans are a wonderful way to save for college (some of us are wondering how this ever got by Congress, given how stingy they've been in raising retirement plan contribution limits). But when it comes to actually setting up your own 529 savings plan, you'll need to go through a financial services firm. Try to find a broker or advisor who is knowledgeable about 529 plans (not all of them are) and who can help you choose a program that meets your needs.

Here are the three main benefits of Section 529 plans:

1. Tax benefits.

The tax deferral works just like your 401(k) and IRA: the earnings in the account build up free from current tax. This benefit is important because it lets you earn investment returns on money you would normally pay Uncle Sam. Then when you take the money out to pay for the child's educational expenses, the withdrawals are tax free.

2. Investment flexibility.

The plans differ considerably from state to state and from one mutual fund sponsor to another in investment flexibility. The mutual fund that I work with chose Rhode Island's plan partly because it places few restrictions on how the assets can be invested. Although it only makes sense to be more aggressive while the child is young and gradually move to more conservative investments as college draws closer, everybody's situation is different. If you're late getting started, you may want to be more aggressive with your 12-year-old's college fund than someone who already has a lot of money saved up. A plan that offers investment flexibility allows you to tailor the portfolio to meet your needs.

3. Estate planning and control.

If you are a young parent struggling to save for your kids' college, you probably don't have enough assets to worry about estate taxes. But your parents might. And this could be a great way to encourage your folks to help out with college. If they are interested in removing assets from their estate for tax purposes, they can each put $10,000 per child per year into a Section 529 plan and, unlike other types of gifts, retain control of the money. It gets complicated, so I won't go into all the details here. But if your parents are concerned about estate taxes, get some help with this. Estate taxes aside, 529 plans lend themselves perfectly to family participation. Set one up when your child is young and encourage all the relatives to put birthday and Christmas gifts into the account.

After-Tax Savings Vehicles

Once you have your retirement plan in place and your college savings plan in place, you'll probably want to start an after-tax savings program for all the vacations, new cars, new furniture, and other indulgences you'll one day be able to afford now that you are not frittering your money away on day-to-day impulse items. Just open an account with a mutual fund company and sign up for their automatic investment program. The amount you specify will be withdrawn from your bank account and invested in whichever type of fund you want. You don't even have to do anything to make this happen. Just be sure to subtract the amount from your check register every month so you won't be in danger of bouncing checks. More on mutual funds in Chapter 8.

IDEAS FOR BOOSTING YOUR SAVINGS

No chapter on saving would be complete without the usual tips on how to free up extra money for saving. It may seem that little things, like taking your lunch two days a week instead of eating out everyday, are meaningless. But they do add up. Save $25 a week on lunches and other incidentals and you'll have $1,300 at the end of the year. Keep it up for another 5 years and you'll have more than $10,000—enough for new living room furniture or a fabulous vacation. In fact, it's by cutting out the little things that you are able to meet your goals without having to make major lifestyle changes. You may need to make some changes in your daily routine, however, in order to remove the temptation to spend.

- **Stay out of the malls.** What you don't see you won't want. If you have to go to the mall, take a list of things you need and stick to it. If shopping is a form of entertainment for you, find other ways of having fun that don't tempt you at every turn. Some of these diversions can even make you a better person, such as reading classic books from the library or learning to play a musical instrument.

- **Throw out the catalogs.** Ditto about not wanting what you don't see. Better yet, save a few trees by asking to have your name removed from the catalog mailing lists.
- **Give yourself an allowance.** Remember when your parents gave you a set amount each week and you had to make it last? Keep up the tradition by withdrawing a set amount from the automatic teller machines and spending no more than this on incidentals. If you have money left over, put it into a kitty for periodic indulgences.
- **Put things on "layaway."** If you tend to be an impulse shopper, make a commitment to wait at least 24 hours before buying something in the "don't have to spend" category. If you're worried the item will be gone when you go back, ask the store to hold it. Chances are, once you've left the store you'll decide it's more important to keep the money.
- **Save all windfalls.** Put all bonus checks, tax refunds, gifts of cash, and other unexpected windfalls immediately into your savings or investment account. You can spend it later—once you've prioritized your goals and made decisions about what's important to you. Again, you're avoiding impulse purchases and spending according to plan. The longer you leave those windfalls invested, the more you'll be able to spend on something you've really been wanting and looking forward to having.

CHAPTER SIX

MAKING YOUR MONEY WORK FOR YOU, PART I

Developing Your Wealth-Building Formula

Money is a terrible master but an excellent servant.

P.T. Barnum

ONCE YOU'VE *EARNED* A LITTLE MONEY, and *saved* a little money, you can make your money start working for you, which is how you really get rich. When investment earnings start building on top of each other, they take on a life of their own and keep growing. Some people think it's the amount you save that determines how wealthy you become. This is only partially true. Although you must provide the seed money for investment earnings to compound, time and investment returns have the ability to turn even modest savings into a big, fat nest egg.

Here's an example of what I mean (see Figure 6-1). If you save $400 per month and earn average investment returns of 8 percent, after one year you'll have $4,980. Of this amount, $4,800 represents your contributions and $180 represents investment earnings. Keep saving the same amount, and after 5 years you'll have $29,390. Of this, $24,000 represents your contribution and $5,390 is investment earnings. After 10 years your nest egg will be worth $73,178; of this $48,000 is your contribution, while $25,178 is investment earnings. After 20 years you'll have $235,608; $96,000 of this represents your total contributions while investment returns represent $139,608. Now you've reached the point where your investment earnings exceed your savings. In that 20th year, when your nest egg is worth $235,608, your annual contribution is still the same $4,800 ($400 per month × 12 months), but now your investment earnings for 1 year total $18,848 ($235,608 × .08). You've gone from making a meager $180 in the first year to more than $18,000 in the 20th year, and you didn't do a thing except make your monthly $400 contributions and keep the money invested in something that returned an average of 8 percent a year.

The classic formula for building wealth is this:

Principal × Rate × Time = Value of your nest egg

Figure 6-1   Breakdown of saved amount and investment earnings if $400 per month is saved and investments earn 8 percent compounded annually. In the later years investment earnings comprise a larger portion of the total amount in savings.

Years	Amount Saved /	Investment Earnings /		Total
1	$4,800	$180	$4,980	
5	$24,000	$5,390	$29,390	
10	$48,000	$25,178	$73,178	
20	$96,000	$139,608	$235,608	

Principal is the amount you put up—$400 per month in the foregoing example. *Rate* is the percentage return your money earns—8 percent in the example. *Time* is just what it says—the amount of time you give your nest egg to grow. This formula is an immutable law. You must have all three components—principal, a rate of return, and time—in order to build wealth. People who buy lottery tickets are trying to circumvent the formula by eliminating the time component and most of the principal component (except for the price of the lottery tickets). People who buy speculative stocks in the hope of tripling their money in a year are trying to compress the time component and are being unrealistic about the rate component. Three hundred percent a year is not a predictable, sustainable rate of return.

THE THREE COMPONENTS OF THE WEALTH-BUILDING FORMULA

The first step in wealth-building is to understand that all three components—principal, rate, and time—must be present. The second step is to understand how you can adjust the components to help you achieve your goals. The third step is to develop reasonable expectations about each of these components so you're not counting on time you don't have or a rate that's unrealistic.

Principal

Principal is the amount on which the rate is applied. If you put $1,000 into a savings account that earns 5 percent compounded annually, your principal is the $1,000. Your interest is calculated by multiplying the principal ($1,000) by the rate (.05) for a total of $50. If you leave the $50 in the account, going into the second year the new principal becomes $1,050. If you continue to leave the earnings in the account, the principal rises by the amount of the earnings for that year and the amount on which the rate is applied gets bigger every year. This is how you build wealth without doing anything. It's how the rich get richer. Don't blame them for amassing huge amounts of money; they can't help it. When your principal is $100 million and you earn a rate of 5 percent, your wealth increases by $5 million a year. And if you can't spend the whole $5 million, whatever's left gets added to the principal and earns another 5 percent the next year. And so on and so on and so on.

Now, you can help the process along by adding to your principal on a regular basis. That's what Chapter 5 was all about: freeing up extra money for savings. By frequently infusing your investment account with new money, you increase the principal component of the wealth-building equation, which affects the final result after the rate and time components are applied. Here's an example of how increasing the principal component and leaving the rate and time components unchanged can affect the outcome.

Start with $1,000, let it compound at 5% for 10 years = $1,647.

Start with $1,000, add $100 per year, let it compound at 5% for 10 years = $2,886.

Start with $1,000, add $1,000 per year, let it compound at 5% for 10 years = $14,206.

Start with $1,000, increase your annual contributions by 10% each year (i.e., $1010 in year 2, $1,111 in year 3, etc.), let it compound at 5% for 10 years = $20,925.

As you can see from this example, increasing your savings every year can significantly impact the end result. So if you're depressed because you're not able to save as much as you'd like to now, just remember that as time goes on you'll likely be able to increase your savings as your salary goes up and you find more ways to cut the fat out of your budget. It's always great to turn over a new leaf all at once, but sometimes leaves have to be turned slowly. Getting a handle on your finances is a huge first step; meeting your ideal savings target may take a little extra time.

Rate

The rate is the percentage of your principal that you earn in investment returns. In the foregoing example it's 5 percent. In other examples throughout this book it's 8 percent. Please note that it is not 12 percent or 15 percent or 25 percent or 100 percent, because rates this high are never predictable in advance. You would never find a financial institution that would promise to pay you 25 percent on your money. The only way to earn a rate this high is by investing in stocks or some other capital asset where the "rate" is actually the amount of increase in the asset's value, which is determined by the marketplace, or what someone else is willing to pay for the asset at the time you are ready to sell. If you buy a stock at $20 per share and sell it a year later at $25, your return would be 25 percent (not counting trading costs). But at the time you bought the stock you couldn't have been sure you would be able to sell it at $25. So it's always safe to count on single-digit returns when planning your savings and investment program.

Of course, your actual investment returns are all that count. It doesn't matter what rate I or any other advisor says is reasonable to expect, because what you actually earn determines what you end up with. To see how the rate component affects the wealth-building formula, let's keep the principal and time components the same and see what the various outcomes would be:

Start with $1,000, let it compound at 5% for 10 years = $1,647.

Start with $1,000, let it compound at 8% for 10 years = $2,159.

Start with $1,000, let it compound at 12% for 10 years = $3,105.

Start with $1,000, let it compound at 15% for 10 years = $4,045.

Obviously, the higher the rate, the more money you will end up with. But to understand where these "rates" come from, you must understand the nature of investments. It's pretty easy to find an account that will promise to pay you a rate of 5 percent. You can even find investments that "promise" to pay you 8 percent. I put "promise" in quotes because there's a slight chance these investments will be unable to fulfill their promise. A corporate bond would be a good example of an investment currently offering an 8 percent return. In all likelihood, the corporation would be able to meet its obligation, but there's always a chance the company could come upon hard times and be unable to meet its interest payments to bondholders. You could even find corporate bonds offering more than 8 percent—some go as high as 10 percent or 11 percent. But these entail more risk—corporations that are on shakier financial footing and in greater danger of not meeting their interest payments. Rate and risk go hand in hand: the higher you go up the rate scale, the higher you must go up the risk scale. (More on this in Chapter 7.)

Once you get above 10 percent or so, your "rate" is determined not by what someone else promises to pay you, but the amount by which a capital asset increases in value. Here you enter the land of the unknown. Because stocks have become such popular investments and because their returns are often stated in percentage terms (e.g., the average annual for the S&P 500 over the last 70 years was 11 percent), it's easy for new investors to think stock market returns are predictable in advance.

Even those who know that stock prices are unpredictable some-times assume mutual fund returns are predictable, even though the mutual funds they're referring to are investing in stocks! They'll see that the average return for a particular growth fund was, say, 12 percent over the last 3 years and assume that after they put their money in they'll make 12 percent as well. But mu-tual fund returns depend on changes in the asset values of the stocks (and/or bonds) in the portfolio. And those asset values are never predictable.

I don't mean to scare you away from investing in stocks or stock mutual funds just because you can't predict what your returns will be. On the contrary. Stocks have a feature that fixed-rate investments do not offer: growth. When you invest in stocks—whether directly or through mutual funds—you are in-vesting in viable companies that are making products and selling them to customers and, hopefully, increasing their revenues and profits every year. As a company's earnings go up, its shares tend to become more valuable. I say "tend to" because share prices don't always move up dollar for dollar with earnings. When in-vestors expect a company's earnings to grow at a fast rate, some-times they bid up the price of the stock in anticipation of those earnings, which is what happened during the Internet bubble. Once investors came to their senses and realized they were pay-ing too much for earnings that hadn't materialized yet (and may never materialize), the stocks dropped in value. So when invest-ing in stocks, you not only want a company whose earnings are growing every year, but one that doesn't carry too high a price tag on those earnings. This aspect of investing is one of the trickiest and is why I generally leave individual stock selection to pro-fessional portfolio managers who spend their days immersed in financial data and are skilled at analyzing it.

Time

Time is what people seem to have so little of these days. Every-body's in a hurry to make money fast, so they look for all kinds of ways to reduce the time component of the wealth-building equation. The paradox is that by fooling around with lotteries and risky stocks and other get-rich-quick schemes, they are wasting precious time that they could be using to make their money grow. The other paradox concerning time is that when you're young and have so much of it on your side, you don't appreciate it. It's only when you get older and realize how little time you have left that you recognize its value. At that point it's easy to become discouraged and think it's useless to try to save money because you aren't able to give it very much time to grow. So here we have young people not saving because they think they have all the time in the world and older people not saving because they think it's already too late, when really *everybody* should be saving in order to take advantage of the time they *do* have left. So whether you're 25 and have your whole career ahead of you or 55 with little or no nest egg saved up, the best time to start saving is *right now*.

Let's look at some examples of how powerful time can be in building wealth.

If you want to build a nest egg of $1 million, here's how to do it (assuming investment returns of 8 percent):

Save $5,466 per month for 10 years.

Save $1,698 per month for 20 years.

Save $670 per month for 30 years.

Save $286 per month for 40 years.

This list shows that by increasing the time element of the wealth-building equation you can reduce the principal component. This point becomes even more dramatic when you add up all your monthly contributions and compare it to the total amount of investment earnings. If you save $286 per month for 40 years, your total contribution is $137,280. The remainder of the $1 million, or $862,720, is investment earnings. Figure 6-2 shows the ratio of contributions to investment earnings for each time period.

Figure 6-2   The value of time. Breakdown of saved amount and investment earnings for different time periods (assumes investment returns of 8% compounded annually).

Years	Amount Saved / Investment Earnings		Total ($1 million)
10	$655,920		$344,080
20	$407,520	$592,480	
30	$241,200	$758,800	
40	$137,280	$826,720	

Each bar shows the two components as follows:

10 years	$655,920 contributions, $344,080 investment returns
20 years	$407,520 contributions, $592,480 investment returns
30 years	$241,200 contributions, $758,800 investment returns
40 years	$137,280 contributions, $862,720 investment returns

As you can see, the more time you give your contributions to compound, the less you need to contribute. Anyone who wants to get rich the easy way ought to let time do most of the work rather than searching for shortcuts that seldom work. That, of course, means starting a savings program as soon as possible and not letting another year go by without planting the seed that gets the compounding going.

WHO'S RICHER, MIKE OR IKE?

Mike and Ike are both 25 years old. Although they are both just starting their careers, Mike is already thinking about retirement and understands the time value of money. He immediately starts saving $400 per month in his company's 401(k) plan. Ten years later, after contributing a total of $48,000, he stops contributing and leaves the money in the plan to grow. Ike, however, waits 10 years to start contributing. He contributes $400 per month for 30 years, or a total of $144,000. When they both turn 65, who do you think has the most money?

If you said "Mike" you're right. Even though Mike contributed far less than Ike, he had more time on his side. Over the 40 years from age 25 to 65, Mike's $48,000 grew to $800,255, while Ike's $144,000 grew to just $596,144. That's because Mike made his contributions early and let time take care of the rest.

FINDING A FORMULA THAT WORKS FOR YOU

The key to making the wealth-building formula work for you is to adjust the variables based on your own personal situation. If you are young and just getting started in your career, you may not be able to make the principal component of your wealth-building formula very large, but you can make up for it by taking advantage of the time portion, that is, by starting to save now, even if it's just a small amount, and keeping the money invested so it will grow. Conversely, if you are in your 50s and by necessity have a smaller time component working for you, you can make up for it by increasing the principal portion. Many people in their 50s are in their peak earning years and have major family expenses behind them so they are able to make up for lost time quickly by stashing away relatively large amounts of their salary.

Everyone must remember, however, that the further away the goal is, the more money you're going to need because inflation will be driving up the goal by 3 percent or 4 percent a year. So while a 60-year-old may be able to retire comfortably today with $1 million, a 30-year-old will need nearly $3 million to retire at the same age with the same standard of living, assuming costs go up by 3.5 percent a year. Young people should not get too complacent about having so much time on their side, because they're going to need it.

Consider Your Age and Life Expectancy

The other thing to keep in mind concerning the time component in retirement planning is that ultimately it relates to life expectancy. Regardless of your age right now and assuming you are not already retired, the rest of your life is divided into two phases. The period between now and retirement is when you make your contributions and invest the funds to grow your nest egg as large as possible. We'll call this Phase 1. Once you crack the nest egg open and start taking income from it, you enter Phase 2. (It doesn't matter if you continue to work during retirement; if you are making withdrawals from your retirement fund, you are in Phase 2.) Phase 2 lasts until you no longer need food, clothing, and shelter—in other words, when you're dead. Now, the fact that none of us knows when we'll die could, if we let it, make financial planning very difficult. After all, whether our retirement fund must last 20 years or 40 years has a huge bearing on how much we'll need at the start of Phase 2. So here's an easy way to do it: Plan on living at least to age 90. (Or use 95 or 100 if you really want to play it safe.) Now all you have to do is subtract your current age from 90 to determine how many years will comprise both Phase 1 and 2. Next, draw the dividing line that separates Phase 1 from Phase 2. Here is an example (see Figure 6-3).

　　Tom is 30 now. If he subtracts his current age from 90, he sees that Phase 1 and 2 together will comprise 60 years. He'd like to retire at 60. That gives him 30 years to build his retirement fund (Phase 1), and 30 years to withdraw income from his nest egg (Phase 2). Now that he knows the time component, he can use a planning calculator (at www.timevalue.com) to determine (1) how much he'll need at the start of Phase 2 to give him the income he'll need for 30 years, and (2) how much he needs to save between now and then to accumulate the necessary funds. If the saving requirement is too onerous, he can adjust the time component by changing his target retirement age to 65. This will give him an extra 5 years to save, increasing Phase 1 to 35 years, and 5 fewer years to draw income, reducing Phase 2 to 25 years. Both

Figure 6-3   Tom's life span broken down into Phase 1 (retirement saving years) and Phase 2 (retirement spending years).

Tom's Original Goal

Current Age		Retirement Age		Life Expectancy
30 years			30 years	
30	Phase 1 (saving)	60	Phase 2 (spending)	90

Tom's Revised Goal

Current Age		Retirement Age		Life Expectancy
35 years			25 years	
30	Phase 1 (saving)	65	Phase 2 (spending)	90

of these adjustments—increasing Phase 1 and reducing Phase 2—will make it easier for Tom to achieve his goal.

The one option that is not open to Tom or anybody else is reducing Phase 2 without increasing Phase 1—in other words, shortening his life expectancy to 85 or 80 or 75 to make his saving job easier. This part of the wealth-building formula is not within our control. Each person's life span will be whatever it is and planning for a short life expectancy won't make saving any easier; it will just leave us destitute in our old age. It is absolutely crucial to be conservative in your life expectancy assumptions. The last thing you want is to run out of money at a time in life when you are least able to earn more.

Consider the Risks

The rate component of the formula is the most difficult to predict, because unless you invest in some fixed-income vehicle that promises a return of x percent, you can never be sure of the exact rate at which your money will grow. And since fixed-income vehicles such as bonds and stable-value accounts generally do not allow for growth over and above the specified rate, I recommend that most people include stocks or stock mutual funds in their portfolios, even though the exact returns from these investments are unpredictable.

The most important thing to understand about the rate component is that if you aim for a high rate, you run the risk of not making it. Let's say you want to reduce both the principal and time components of your formula by increasing the rate portion. You see from your calculator that by increasing the rate to 12 percent, you can compile $1 million much easier and faster than in the previous examples, which are based on an 8 percent rate. If your savings average a 12 percent annual return, you could compile $1 million this way:

> Save $4,347 per month for 10 years (instead of $5,466 at 8 percent).
>
> Save $1,010 per month for 20 years (instead of $1,698 at 8 percent).
>
> Save $286 per month for 30 years (instead of $670 at 8 percent).
>
> Save $85 per month for 40 years (instead of $286 at 8 percent).

Or, let's look at it another way. If you were to save the same amounts indicated in the 8 percent examples, you could compile even more than $1 million:

> Save $5,466 per month @ 12 percent for 10 years = $1,257,392.
>
> Save $1,698 per month @ 12 percent for 20 years = $1,679,755.
>
> Save $670 per month @ 12 percent for 30 years = $2,341,625.
>
> Save $286 per month @ 12 percent for 40 years = $3,364,725.

Based purely on these calculations, a person would be crazy to accept the 8 percent rate plan when she could compile more money and do it easier and faster with the 12 percent rate plan. That's why it is vital to remember that these "rate plans" are based on assumptions only. Accepting the 12 percent rate plan does not ensure that you will earn 12 percent. It only changes the savings requirement and lets you off the hook for saving the higher amount. But if you end up not earning the 12 percent, you will be in danger of having saved too little.

I must restate another excruciatingly obvious fact: The rate you actually earn determines the amount you eventually end up with. This is especially important to keep in mind when visiting financial advisors. Just because an advisor bases your financial plan on a rate of 10 percent or 12 percent doesn't mean he or she can actually achieve that for you. Needless to say, this concept also applies to brokers you meet at parties who promise to double your money in a year. I use conservative assumptions for my clients so they will be sure to save enough when planning for major long-term goals such as college and retirement. If they end up earning more than 8 percent, the surprises will be on the upside: They can either retire sooner, or retire with more money, or cut back on the amount they need to save.

The biggest danger in basing your assumptions on a high rate is that it might cause you to save too little if reality doesn't match your assumptions. The other danger is that it may influence your investment strategy and lead you into risky investments, which means you may not only fail to achieve your targeted rate of return, you could actually end up losing money. The kinds of investments that offer the potential to earn a high rate of return are not safe bets. But if you're feeling pressured to earn a high rate in order to meet your goals, you might be tempted to subject your hard-earned principal to unusually high risk. Aiming for a more reasonable goal of 8 percent gives you many more investments to choose from, enables you to be more conservative in your investing, and, in the end, sleep better at night.

DEVELOPING REASONABLE EXPECTATIONS
FOR YOUR WEALTH-BUILDING FORMULA

In Chapter 5 we explained how to establish a savings plan. This plan determines the principal component of your wealth-building formula. Obviously, the more principal you can provide, the more wealth you can accumulate. You may be limited by circumstances (too little income, too many bills) right now, but understanding how your savings fit into the formula may inspire you to squeak a few more dollars out of your budget for saving. By keeping in mind that your principal is aided by investment returns and time to build a much bigger fund than if you had to rely on savings alone, you'll be more inclined to get started. The principal is the catalyst for the whole thing; without it, rate and time have nothing to act on.

Tie It to Your Goals

Chapter 3 discussed goal setting and Figure 3-1 included a column for "date needed." The date needed will help you determine the time component of your wealth-building formula. Actually, you may have several formulas. If you're like most people, you have many different goals with many different target dates. An easy way to keep them all straight is to develop a different formula for each goal and integrate them all with your savings plan. As noted in Chapter 5, if your goals exceed your ability to save for them, some adjustments need to be made, by either scaling back the goals or finding extra money for saving. By making a wealth-building formula for each goal, you can pinpoint the amount you need to save. Don't try this without a calculator. Go to www.timevalue.com or use the investment calculator that came with your personal finance software package (Quicken or Microsoft Money) if you have one. One benefit of these calculators is that you can inflate the contributions. For example, let's say you wanted to have $100,000 in 10 years. If you were to save a fixed amount over the 10 years, you'd have to save $547 per month. But if you were to increase your savings by 10 percent a year, you could start out saving just $342 per month. It's entirely reasonable to expect that your income will rise in the years ahead and that as you retire current debt you'll be able to apply those payments to your savings plan.

Here are some sample goals and the wealth-building formula needed to achieve them, as determined by the calculator.

Goal #1: Retirement

Amount needed: $2 million

Target date: 30 years

Wealth-building formula: Save $374 per month @ 8 percent for 30 years; increase savings by 10 percent a year.

Goal #2: Establish an emergency fund

Amount needed: $15,000

Target date: 1 year

Wealth-building formula: Save $1,216 per month @ 6 percent* for one year

Goal #3: Save for down payment on a house

Amount needed: $30,000

Target date: 5 years

Wealth-building formula: Save $337 per month @ 6 percent for 5 years; increase savings by 10 percent per year.

When you add up these savings amounts, they may be more than you can handle all at once. Goal #2, the emergency fund, is a rather aggressive goal—$15,000 in one year—so you may want to get that out of the way before you start on goal #3. However, you should not delay retirement saving for any reason. This example shows a saving requirement of $374 per month for retirement in 30 years. If you put it off just 5 years, your saving requirement jumps to $707 per month.

*I use 6 percent for any goal less than 5 years away.

Understand Investment Returns and
the Markets That Determine Them

Although the principal and time components of your wealth-building formula vary depending on your circumstances and how you choose to construct them, the rate component will remain the same: 6 percent for goals less than 5 years away, and 8 percent for goals longer than 5 years. You may be wondering how I came up with those numbers, especially since I already said investment returns that involve capital assets such as stocks are unpredictable in advance. You may also think these numbers sound awfully low. After all, you've probably had conversations with people who've made 50 percent or 100 percent on their stocks. If you pay attention to the stock reports, you may have heard that in 1999 the S&P 500 was up 21 percent and the Nasdaq was up a whopping 89 percent. You may even have visited Microsoft's Web site that shows how much your investment would be worth today if you had invested in the company when it first went public in 1986. A $2,100 investment (100 shares at $21) would, as of this writing, be worth $864,000 (14,400 shares at $60) for a compound annual return of nearly 49 percent.

You've probably already heard numbers like these, or something close to them, which is why you think my 6 percent and 8 percent assumptions are ridiculously low. So allow me to explain why the numbers you may have heard from your stock market friends and the media do not represent the real world.

First, they only tell one side of the story. Yes, the S&P 500 was up 21 percent in 1999, but it was down 9 percent in 2000. Yes, the Nasdaq was up 86 percent in 1999, but it was down 39 percent in 2000. Yes, Microsoft has richly rewarded its shareholders since its initial public offering (IPO) in 1986, but hundreds of companies have either gone belly up or are trading significantly below their offering prices. Whenever you hear stories of someone else's investment success, you must put the information in perspective and understand that you are hearing about one tiny slice of market activity; it has no bearing whatsoever on the larger investment picture. You also must consider the source and what the person's motive is in telling you the story. Is it to gain your respect? Sell magazines? One thing is for sure: It's probably not to help you gain a realistic sense of potential investment returns so you can plan your financial future.

Second, the numbers are not dealing with an entire portfolio. It's human nature for people to talk about their winners and keep quiet about their losers. The next time someone brags about the killing she made on a stock, ask her how her whole portfolio did. She probably won't even know. When you read about stocks or mutual funds in the financial magazines, again remember that you are looking at one investment, not a whole portfolio that has been carefully constructed to balance risk and return based on your individual needs.

Third, the numbers are from isolated time periods. The media and the investment industry tend to discuss investment performance on a calendar year basis, which is like taking a long motion picture and chopping it up into individual frames. While it allows you to scrutinize each frame, it does not allow you to understand what the whole movie is about. One of the reasons they do this is so they can compare one investment against another or against a particular benchmark such as the S&P 500 for the specific time period. While this approach has some value when you are comparing mutual funds, for example, it is of no value at all when you are trying to plan your saving and investing strategy over an entire lifetime.

Why It's Reasonable to Expect Single-Digit Investment Returns

Let me explain why I think it's reasonable to plan for 6 percent returns for short-term investments and 8 percent for long-term investments.

Before I get into the market data, the first reason relates to your own happiness and well-being. I would rather have you pleasantly surprised by higher-than-expected returns than disappointed by lower-than-expected results. Also, I want to make sure you save enough. If you base your savings requirements on a 12 percent return and don't make it, you'll have to make some serious adjustments to your goals just when you were hoping to enjoy them. There's nothing worse than looking forward to retiring at age 60 only to discover when you get there that you have to keep working another 5 years. And then there's the matter of your emotional peace and well-being during your investment journey. I want you to be able to sleep at night and not worry about your investments or about your children's college or your own retirement.

These reasons should be enough to take my advice about lowering your return expectations, but here are a few more based on my 20 years of experience in the investment industry and my current observations of the markets.

THE 1990S WERE AN ABERRATION

If you only started looking at the stock market in the 1990s, you have had a very unrealistic view of stock market performance. During this time, stock prices appreciated far more than usual, partly because corporate earnings were growing at a rapid pace due to the extraordinary economic expansion, but also because of what's called *multiple expansion*. In 1990 stocks (as measured by the S&P 500) were selling at an average of 15 times earnings. By the end of the decade they were selling at over 25 times earnings. Throughout the decade, investors kept placing a higher and higher value on corporate earnings, and this change in investor perceptions—not actual earnings increases—accounted for much of the rise in stock prices. Not only has multiple expansion pretty much run its course, it's probably just a matter of time before it starts going the other way and heading back down to its historical average. I don't have to tell you this could signal a drop in stock prices.

The long-term (70-year) average annual return for stocks is about 11 percent. From 1995 through 1999, the S&P 500 averaged more than 28 percent. Statisticians use a term called *reversion to the mean* to describe an adjustment that brings something back to its historical average. Under this argument, it would take 5 years of negative returns to balance out the 1995–1999 aberration and bring overall returns back to their 11 percent historical average. Again, I don't mean to scare you away from stocks. I'm just trying to show you a balanced picture, because I've seen too many people make huge mistakes due to unrealistic expectations.

THERE'S MORE TO INVESTING THAN STOCKS

A diversified, balanced portfolio should have a mix of stocks for growth, bonds for income and stability, and cash for liquidity. Warren Buffett and other rich investors may like to place big bets on a handful of well-researched companies, but ordinary people who are saving for college and retirement can't afford to do that. The consequences of being wrong are just too great. So we include some lower-yielding investments along with our stocks, knowing full well they are lower yielding but appreciating their other benefits, such as income, stability, and liquidity. When you have a mix of stocks (whose returns have averaged 11 percent), bonds (with historical average returns of about 6 percent) and money market funds (currently yielding about 4 percent), you can see that your average return for the whole portfolio will be in the range of 7 percent to 10 percent, depending on the mix. What really matters, of course, is not how these investments have performed in the past, but how they will do in the future. Coming off an extraordinary decade for stocks and the current indications of a slowing economy, I see every reason to proceed with caution. Specific investment strategies are discussed in Chapters 7 and 8.

CHAPTER SEVEN

MAKING YOUR MONEY WORK FOR YOU, PART II

Creating an Asset Allocation Plan

Don't gamble! Take all your savings and buy some good stock and hold it till it goes up, then sell it. If it don't go up, don't buy it.

Will Rogers

THERE'S A BIG DIFFERENCE between gambling and investing. Because the same vehicles (stocks) are often used for both, it can be easy to mix them up and think you're investing when you're really gambling and vice versa. But the distinction is really quite easy to discern. What determines whether you're gambling or investing is the groundwork you lay (or not) before you ever put a dime into a stock.

Gambling—also called speculating—is when you buy a stock without regard to any of the other issues we've been talking about in this book: your goals, your time horizon (when you'll need the money), your asset mix (stocks, bonds, cash), and—something we haven't talked about yet—your risk tolerance. The gambler isn't thinking about his overall financial situation and how to build wealth in a predictable, methodical manner. He (or she) just wants to make a lot of money fast. The financial magazines encourage this approach by featuring cover blurbs like "Ten hot stocks to buy now!" Your friends encourage it when they brag about their latest stock find. Some stockbrokers encourage it when they give you stock ideas without understanding your overall financial situation and what you are trying to accomplish. People who act on these isolated stock picks without looking at their overall financial plan are gambling, not investing. And as you know, gambling can be very, very risky.

WHAT'S YOUR RISK TOLERANCE?

Risk tolerance is a funny thing. Whenever I ask new clients about their risk tolerance, everyone says they want to make a lot of money without losing any. Of course. That's the whole idea behind wealth building—to make money and not lose any. When I explain that investments offering the potential for higher returns entail more risk than those guaranteeing a stable principal and a fixed rate, their reactions vary depending on what's been going on in the markets. When I first entered the investment business in the early 1980s, people still had vivid memories of the 1973–74 bear market when the stock market dropped more than 40 percent over a 2-year period. (Some even recalled the crash of 1929, so devastating was the aftermath for people who lived during the Great Depression of the 1930s.) People were afraid of stocks, and when I asked about risk tolerance, most clients said they wanted their money to be safe, even if it meant missing out on the opportunity to earn higher returns. As recently as the mid-1990s most people were still telling me this: Yes, we'll be happy with returns of 8–10 percent if it means we won't have to subject our money to too much risk.

Then in the second half of the 1990s, the stock market took off. The S&P 500 rose 23 percent in 1996, 33 percent in 1997, 28 percent in 1998, and 21 percent in 1999. Eight percent was starting to look like peanuts, especially to people who had been talking to friends who'd doubled or tripled their money in one or two stocks. Then when I would ask clients about their risk tolerance, they would say "Go for it—we want to make a lot of money and yeah, okay, if you say we might lose some, we don't care; we just want to get rich." They didn't really mean this, of course. Nobody wants to lose money, especially people who are intent on getting rich. What they were really saying is they didn't *think* they would lose money. Stocks were going only one way, and they couldn't imagine them dropping. So it was easy for them to say they could handle a 20 percent decline in the value of their portfolio, because they didn't really think it would happen. How do I know this? Because people who said they could handle a 20 percent decline started freaking out when some of their stocks dropped 5 percent.

Meanwhile, clients who were not swayed by stories of friends quadrupling their money in a month were fine when the market started falling in 2001. We had already discussed the possibility of stocks fluctuating in value, and so they knew it was part of the program. By staying the course—not expecting an unrealistically high return and understanding the realities of risk—they were in much better shape to carry on. But the people who had cashed in some of their mutual funds to buy high-flying stocks overreacted when the stocks came tumbling down. Now gun-shy, they didn't want their old investments back, they wanted supersafe bonds and cash. On the risk tolerance scale, they went from one extreme to the other practically overnight.

Don't Know Your Risk Tolerance? You're Not Alone

Risk tolerance is a very complicated matter. Most people don't even know what their risk tolerance is. It's hard to imagine how you'd feel if your portfolio were to drop 10 percent or 20 percent if it's never happened to you before. Would you panic and sell? Would you take it all in stride? Would you leave your portfolio alone but stay awake nights worrying about it? It's hard to know what you'd do. One thing studies have shown for sure is that investors who work with a financial advisor tend to worry less about interim losses and are less likely to make radical moves in response to market movements. This statement is not just a commercial for working with an advisor. Several studies have shown that mutual fund investors who do not work with an advisor tend to switch in and out of funds at the wrong time, causing them to end up with lower returns than if they'd stayed in the same funds. Hand holding is part of my job, and it seems to have a positive impact on investment returns as well as my clients' sense of comfort and well-being.

A very important part of risk tolerance is your time horizon. If you plan to start writing tuition checks in 3 years, you'll want to make sure the money you have saved is all there when you need it. However, if you're investing for retirement in 30 years, you can take stock market fluctuations in stride because you have plenty of time to make up the losses. Your time horizon should dictate how you invest, as well as how you react emotionally to fluctuations in value. Any money you plan to spend within 5 years should be in a money market fund or short-term bond fund; that in itself will spare you emotional agony because losses are out of the question. If you are nervous about fluctuations in your retirement fund, you can talk yourself out of it by remembering that you won't be needing the money for many years.

Another important aspect to risk tolerance is return potential. If you assume that risk and return go hand in hand, you can gauge your risk tolerance by thinking about how much you want your portfolio to earn. Clearly, it doesn't make sense to aim for 10 percent or 12 percent if you can't stand to see your portfolio fluctuate in value. Something has to give; either you need to lower your return expectation or raise your risk tolerance. To give you an idea of the range of volatility, Table 7-1 shows the best and worst years for the various asset classes. Reviewing this table will prepare you for the discussion on asset allocation that follows.

Risk Tolerance Questionnaire

Despite the dynamic, complicated nature of risk tolerance, investors seem to like questionnaires that help them assess their attitudes about risk. Here is a simple one that applies to money you won't need for at least 5 years. Try to be as honest as possible.

1. Which category best matches your attitude toward investment risk?
    a. I am very comfortable with risk and willing to take more risk over longer periods of time to pursue maximum growth.
    b. I am not comfortable with risk, but I am willing to accept some risk in order to increase the value of my portfolio over time.
    c. I am very uncomfortable with investment risk.
2. What is the most you could stand to see your investment portfolio drop in value in any one year?
    a. More than 20 percent
    b. 6 percent to 20 percent
    c. 5 percent or less
3. What would you do if your portfolio suddenly dropped by 10 percent?
    a. Nothing, as long as I still believed my investments had good long-term potential.
    b. Worry a little, but not take any action.
    c. Bail out and go to cash.

Table 7-1   Range of Volatility for Asset Classes, 1986–2000

	Best Year	Worst Year
Large Growth[a]	+38.7% (1998)	–22.4% (2000)
Large Value[b]	+38.4% (1995)	–8.1% (1990)
Mid Growth[c]	+51.3% (1999)	–11.8% (2000)
Mid Value[d]	+34.9% (1995)	–16.1% (1990)
Small Growth[e]	+51.2% (1991)	–22.4% (2000)
Small Value[f]	+31.8% (1997)	–21.8% (1990)
International[g]	+69.9% (1986)	–23.2% (1990)
S&P 500[h]	+37.6% (1995)	–9.1% (2000)
Cash (Treasury bills)	+8.4% (1989)	+3.51% (1992)
Inflation	6.1% (1990)	1.6% (1998)

[a]Large Growth—The Russell 1000 Growth contains those securities in the Russell 1000 with a greater-than-average growth orientation.

[b]Large Value—The Russell 1000 Value contains those securities in the Russell 1000 with less-than-average growth orientation.

[c]Mid Growth—Contains those securities in the Russell Mid Cap (a mid-cap index) with greater-than-average growth orientation.

[d]Mid Value—The Russell Mid Value contains those securities in the Russell Mid Cap (a mid-cap index) with less-than-average growth orientation.

[e]Small Growth—The Russell 2000 Growth contains those securities in the Russell 2000 (a small-cap index) with greater-than-average growth orientation.

[f]Small Value—The Russell 2000 Value contains those securities in the Russell 2000 (a small-cap index) with less-than-average growth orientation.

[g]International—the EAFE index is a market capitalization index that includes over 1,053 stocks from Europe, Australia, New Zealand, and the Far East (including Japan, which equals approximately 45 percent of the index).

[h]S&P 500—Capitalization-weighted benchmark that tracks broad-based changes in the U.S. market. The index is calculated on a total return basis with dividends reinvested.

Give yourself 2 points for each "a" answer, 1 point for each "b" answer, and 0 points for each "c" answer.

If you scored 5 or 6, your risk tolerance is HIGH.

If you scored 2–4, your risk tolerance is MODERATE.

If you scored 0 or 1, your risk tolerance is LOW.

Keep your risk tolerance in mind as we discuss asset allocation.

ASSET ALLOCATION

It's human nature, when you finally get a little money together, to search for a place to put it. So you take your few hundred dollars and find a mutual fund that accepts small initial investments. Then you save up another few hundred dollars and either put it into the same mutual fund or find another one because you know diversification is a good thing. Because your investment funds are becoming available step-by-step, you do your investing step-by-step, putting one foot in front of the other without really thinking about where you're going. This procedure is a hard way to invest, because you have to look for a new investment each time you have some money, and with the markets changing all the time, it's easy to become confused (let's see tech stocks were good last month, but this month they don't look so good; where shall I put my money now?).

Not only does this step-by-step approach require constant decision making, it's easy to end up with a portfolio that's either too concentrated in one investment or overly diversified among too many, all chosen without rhyme or reason. In any case, you end up with a portfolio you don't feel very confident about, because you can't remember the rationale by which it came together. That makes it very hard to manage, especially when the market hits a rocky period and you're wondering whether you should make major changes or keep everything where it is.

I can save you some agony by suggesting a strategy used by very successful investors. It's called an asset allocation plan. With this strategy you decide from the outset which asset classes to invest in, even if you can't do it all at once. This plan serves as your investing guide, so as you accumulate more money you know where to put it. A good analogy would be the blueprints used to build a house. You would never just start building one room and then adding another and another without knowing in advance how the whole house would come together. With an asset allocation plan you'll know how your portfolio will look once you've completed the plan, even if it takes a while to do it. As more money becomes available, you keep adding it to the portfolio according to the proportions indicated in the plan.

Understanding the Attributes of the Various Investments

Quick—why are you investing? If you said "to make money," congratulations. That's the answer everyone gives when they are first embarking on an investment program. The problem is that there are so many investments to choose from and so much that can happen that you need to fine-tune your answer a bit. Here are the attributes that investment portfolios generally have in varying proportions. Designing an asset allocation plan means emphasizing these attributes to different degrees, depending on your risk tolerance, time horizon, and liquidity needs.

GROWTH

Growth is what you get when a capital asset appreciates in value, in other words, when you buy low and sell high. Or when you invest in a mutual fund that buys low and sells high (more on mutual funds in Chapter 8). Growth is a wonderful thing because it means your money is, well, growing. If you start the year with $10,000 and end the year with $11,000, that's growth. There's just one problem with investments whose primary attribute is growth: You can never know in advance how much that growth will be or even if the investment will grow at all. Investments offering growth fluctuate in value. This fluctuation is a good thing when it is on the upside, because that's how you make money. But when it's on the downside, that's not growth at all. It's a loss.

And whenever your portfolio fluctuates on the downside, it has to appreciate that much more to make up the loss.

For example, going from $10,000 to $11,000 is a 10 percent gain. Going from $11,000 to $12,000 is a 9 percent gain. But going from $10,000 down to $7,000 and up to $12,000 is a 30 percent loss followed by a 71 percent gain. It's much harder to find an investment with the potential to earn 71 percent than one offering 9 percent. So the key to investing for growth is to avoid large losses and to take your growth in smaller doses. Your asset allocation plan helps you do that. The higher your risk tolerance and the longer your time horizon, the more growth investments you should have. Because you have plenty of time to withstand interim fluctuations and because inflation will erode the purchasing power of your dollars, you need more growth to make up for it. The classic growth investments are stocks, discussed in the next section.

INCOME

Investments that generate ongoing income are less likely to appreciate in value, but they do throw off a predictable income stream that helps stabilize the portfolio. With income-oriented investments, you always have new money coming into the portfolio, even if you choose not to take actual receipt of the income but rather reinvest it back into the same or another investment. Once the money hits the account, it's yours, in contrast to growth investments, whose appreciation may be on paper only and could easily be taken away by the vagaries of the stock market. The disadvantage to income-oriented investments is that they do not offer the high returns that growth-oriented investments do. However, they do allow you to sleep at night. Bonds are the classic income investment. More on these in the next section.

LIQUIDITY

The term *liquidity* simply means your investment is readily convertible into cash. By this broad definition, most stocks and bonds could be considered liquid investments. But we usually use the term to refer to money market funds or some other safe account that will allow you not only to get your hands on your money in a hurry, but to do it without risk to your principal. As I've noted several times, your emergency fund and any money you plan to spend within 5 years should focus on liquidity by remaining in a money market fund or short-term bond fund. However, liquidity also has a place in a long-term investment portfolio. If you're uncertain about the stock market and don't want to invest all your available funds at once, you can keep some in a liquid account awaiting the right time to buy. The advantage to liquidity is that your money is always there and can be accessed whenever you need it. The disadvantage is that the returns tend to be quite low, often not even keeping up with inflation.

Understanding Your Objectives

TIME HORIZON AND RISK TOLERANCE

When it comes to deciding what percentage of your portfolio should go into growth versus income investments, you should consider two main factors: your time horizon and your risk tolerance. Usually, these go hand-in-hand: People with short time horizons (i.e., those close to retirement) score low on the risk tolerance questionnaire; they naturally feel nervous about risk because they know they have a limited time to make up any losses. However, sometimes people with long time horizons score low on the questionnaire and vice versa. When this happens, your time horizon should rule. That's because financial reality trumps nerves. People with a long time horizon *should* take some risks in order to keep their money growing ahead of inflation, whether their stomachs can handle interim fluctuations or not. Conversely, people with a short time horizon, even if volatile markets don't bother them, need to be somewhat careful.

Keep in mind that your time horizon doesn't end on the day you retire. If you're 50 now and plan to retire at 60 and live to 90, your time horizon is 40 years, not 10. While it's usually a good idea to invest more conservatively when you retire (because your main source of income—your salary—will stop), you shouldn't immediately sell all your stocks and put everything into fixed-income or stable-value investments. Your portfolio will need to keep up with inflation because your income needs will increase in the years ahead. That means keeping some money in growth investments, or stocks.

RETURN EXPECTATIONS

Your return expectations will also have a bearing on your asset mix. I'm not talking about the greed factor but rather the size of your portfolio in relation to your goals. If you are pretty well set with a sizable portfolio or the ability to save a substantial amount every month—in other words, you're on track to easily achieve your goals using an 8 percent return assumption—you don't have to take more risk than you need to. You can take a balanced approach between growth and income. On the other hand, if you've maximized your savings and adjusted your goals and still found that an 8 percent return will not get you where you want to be, the only choice left is to try to increase your return by investing most or all of your portfolio for growth and forgoing the income component of a typical asset allocation plan.

CHANGING MARKET CONDITIONS

Before giving some examples of asset allocation plans, I must throw one more consideration into the mix: The outlook for the economy and the markets. This does *not* mean trying to time the market and pulling all your money out of stocks if the market takes a dive. It means taking advantage of market conditions to maximize returns while minimizing risk. For example, there are times when bonds offer growth potential in addition to their income component. This happens when we're in a period of falling interest rates (I'll explain why in the next section). At these times you might want to switch some of your money from stocks to bonds in order to capture that profit potential. Another example is when the economy is sluggish for an extended period of time during which the more conservative income-oriented investments offer better returns. If all this sounds too complicated, don't worry. You don't have to keep moving your money around to keep up with changing economic market conditions. It's just a way for active investors to enhance their returns if they are so inclined (and may be another reason to work with an advisor, since advisors usually do stay on top of changing market conditions and can suggest when it may be time to shift your asset allocation).

THE THREE MAIN ASSET CLASSES

Instead of talking about the *attributes* of the various investments—growth, income, and liquidity—I'm going to refer to the asset classes by their real names: stocks, bonds, and cash. You'll discover when we get to mutual funds in Chapter 8 that we'll need to go back to talking about growth, income, and such terms, because that's how the funds refer to themselves. (I suppose from a marketing standpoint they want you to think your money will "grow" as opposed to being in stocks, which a lot of people don't understand anyway.) But in order to manage an investment program on an ongoing basis, and especially in order to make sense of mutual funds and their marketing-oriented terminology, it is absolutely essential that you understand the raw nature of investments and the real terminology that goes along with them. Then you will be in a much better position to evaluate investment products (such as mutual funds), or even invest directly in the securities themselves.

So now I will explain the asset classes so that brand-new investors will understand but without putting seasoned investors to sleep. In case I miss something, you can turn to Chapter 10, which features answers to commonly asked questions. If you are simply too bored for words, skip over to the section headed Three-Step Asset Allocation Process.

Stocks

Remember the story from Chapter 2 about Bill Gates and Paul Allen forming a little company they called Microsoft? Because

Microsoft primarily dealt with "soft" wares as opposed to "hard" assets requiring factories and machines, Bill and Paul didn't need a lot of capital to start their company. Their main resource was in their heads: the ability to write lines of computer language (called "code") and sell it to companies (primarily IBM) and individuals who used it in their personal computers. Microsoft could have remained a small, privately owned company forever, just like your local dry cleaner. But when Steve Ballmer joined the company, he had big plans for turning Microsoft into a much bigger company. This meant hiring more people, building offices to put all the people in, and spending lots of money on marketing and advertising to make Microsoft's products well known. Companies that have big plans for growth need more money than they can get from annual sales revenue. One way to get this needed capital is to borrow it. Remember this for the discussion on bonds that follows. Another way to get it is to sell shares of the company to the public. These shares are commonly referred to as *stock*.

On March 13, 1986, Microsoft had its initial public offering (IPO) wherein it issued 2,795,000 shares of the company to the public at $21 per share. Collectively, investors forked over a total of $58,295,000 (2,795,000 shares x $21 per share). After the investment bankers took their cut ($3,661,450), and the selling stockholders (Bill, Paul, and several others) got their share ($15,653,550) Microsoft received a total of $39,380,000 for "general corporate purposes, principally working capital, product development, and capital expenditures" as indicated in the prospectus. Microsoft's first prospectus, by the way, can provide an excellent education in corporate finance. You can download it at http://www.microsoft.com/msft/sec.htm. A prospectus is the document that is filed with the Securities and Exchange Commission whenever a company issues securities to the public; it tells all about the business and includes detailed financial information. (Mutual fund prospectuses also contain important disclosure information; more on these in Chapter 8.)

People invest in stocks primarily to profit from the company's increasing earnings. As the company makes more money, its stock becomes more valuable. That certainly has been the case with Microsoft. After the stock went public at $21 on March 13, 1986, its share price rose to $114.50 on September 18, 1987. To make the stock more affordable for investors, Microsoft *split* the stock 2 for 1. This split meant existing shareholders received an equal number of shares, each worth half as much. So if you had bought 100 shares at $21 on the offering (invested $2,100), your postsplit holdings would be 200 shares at $53.50, or $10,700. Microsoft has split its stock a total of eight times. If you'd held your original 100 shares all that time, you'd now have 14,400 shares. (Please understand that Microsoft is a very unusual case. Most companies don't grow that fast and their stock prices do not go up as much.)

Microsoft has never paid a *dividend*. A dividend is a portion of earnings that some companies pay out to shareholders. In the old days, that was the main reason to invest in stocks; to invest in a non-dividend-paying company was considered speculation. Over the years, however, the trend has been for growth companies to reinvest all of their earnings back into the company. Investors seem fine with this because as long as the company's earnings are increasing their shares are becoming more valuable.

What causes share prices to go up and down? Basically, it's the law of supply and demand. It's also somewhat mysterious. Fundamentally, share prices are supposed to be tied to corporate earnings: As a company earns more money, its shares should become more valuable. But on a day-to-day basis, stock prices jump up and down for no apparent reason. For more information on how stocks trade and how to value stocks based on their earnings, see Chapter 10.

Bonds

The other primary way companies obtain capital for growth is to borrow it. Companies with big borrowing needs can't rely only on banks and other lending institutions. For large borrowings they turn to the public capital markets and issue bonds. You give them some cash, they give you some bonds, sort of like IOUs that serve as evidence of the loan. Each bond is in $1,000 increments. So if you invest $10,000, you get 10 bonds. Each bond spells out the terms of the deal. The *par value*, or *principal* amount is $1,000; this is also called the *face amount*. The *coupon* or *interest rate* is the amount the corporation (called the *issuer*) pays you for the privilege of borrowing your money, like the interest you pay on your credit card balance, except it's usually a lot lower (currently around 7 percent or 8 percent), and the corporation usually does not pay off the principal little by little as you do on your credit card balance. With most bonds, the company pays interest only during the entire *term*, or *duration*. The *maturity date* is the date the company gives you your original investment back.

Here's how bonds work: You invest $10,000 in 10 XYZ 7 percent of 2022. The 10 refers to how many bonds you're buying: ten bonds at $1,000 each. XYZ is the name of the issuing corporation. Seven percent is the interest rate, which works out to $700 per year on your $10,000 (you'll probably get two checks a year for $350 each). You get your $10,000 back in the year 2022. Oh, I can hear you now. *"What if I need my money sooner than 2022? Twenty years is a long time to tie up $10,000."* Lucky for you, bonds trade on the open market just like stocks, so if you want to sell your bonds and get your money back, all you have to do is call your friendly broker and enter a sell order.

Selling the bonds is easy. There's an active and liquid market for most bonds and you can usually have your money within a few days. What isn't so easy is understanding that you may receive more or less than your $10,000 if you sell your bonds prior to maturity. What determines how much you get is where interest rates are at the time you sell. Let's say that after you buy your bonds, interest rates go up and new bonds coming out are paying 8 percent. No one would pay you $1,000 for your 7 percent bonds when they could get 8 percent bonds for the same price. So the price of your bond will be discounted to a price that makes the $70 interest payment equal to an 8 percent interest rate, or roughly $885 per bond. On ten bonds that would give you net proceeds of $8,850. This discounting is how you can lose money in bonds. You can also make money in bonds. If interest rates go the other way, say interest rates go to 6 percent, your 7 percent bonds will be worth more, approximately $1,150 per bond, or $11,500 on your $10,000 investment. If you sell, you'll collect the profit on the bond (the difference between what you paid and what you received, called a *capital gain*) as well as whatever interest you received during the time you owned the bond.

Although it may be easy to say that stocks are always for growth and bonds are always for income, once you understand the nuances of how these securities behave, it's not always so cut and dried. Some corporations pay big, fat dividends to shareholders and because their earnings aren't growing very fast, their stock prices don't appreciate very much; these kinds of stocks are better for income than growth. Also, we've been talking about common stocks here; there's also a class of stock called *preferred stocks* that pay rather large dividends to shareholders, almost as much as bonds pay in interest. And as we've seen, bonds are not always just for income. When interest rates drop, bond prices jump, making bonds a good investment for growth during periods of declining rates.

Cash

When I refer to cash, it generally means a money market fund. Most people think of these as savings accounts, and in some ways they are similar in that you can get at your money quickly. However, money market funds are really big portfolios of very short-term securities (like bonds, but maturing in 30 days or less), which are professionally managed in a way that enables you to redeem your shares at anytime for $1 per share. Money market funds are not insured by the government the way savings accounts are, but to my knowledge no one has ever lost money in a money market fund. In a long-term asset allocation plan, cash (i.e., money market funds) has a unique place and is generally used as a temporary parking place for money that will eventually find its way into stocks or bonds. You might keep some of your long-term money in cash if you recently came into a lump sum and don't want to invest it all at once for fear the market may head down after you've taken the plunge. For example, if let's say you make your profit-sharing Keogh contribution all at once just before your tax filing deadline. You could have as much as $35,000 coming into the account at one time, so rather than putting it all into stocks and bonds according to your asset allocation plan, you ease into the markets by putting the $35,000 into a money market fund and moving $5,000 per month into stocks and bonds. You don't have to do this. You could go ahead and invest the $35,000 in stocks and bonds as soon as it comes into the account. This illustration is simply designed to point out the purpose of cash in a long-term asset allocation plan. Our main focus on the asset allocation discussion that follows is on stocks and bonds.

The investment strategy I recommend makes use of mutual funds (or private portfolio managers if you have more than $100,000), but in a way that gives you much more control over the process. First you decide which asset classes you want to invest in and in what proportion. Then you find the mutual funds that will carry out your plan. This strategy also allows you to ease into the process and to even let the mutual funds do some of your asset allocation work if you don't feel comfortable yet doing it yourself. Meanwhile, you'll be learning a lot about investing.

THREE-STEP ASSET ALLOCATION PROCESS

The first step in the process is to decide how much to invest in stocks versus bonds. The second step divides the stock portion among several subcategories. The third step divides the bond portion among several bond subcategories.

Step One: Decide How Much to Put in Stocks versus Bonds

Assuming your emergency fund and money for short-term goals are safely tucked away, the first step in the asset allocation process is to decide how much of your long-term portfolio to invest in stocks and bonds. Here are some examples:

Scott is single, 30 years old, and wants to retire in 25 years. His risk tolerance is high. Since he has very little saved, he wants to maximize returns. He allocates 100 percent of his portfolio to stocks.

Julie is also single, also 30 years old, and also wants to retire in 25 years. Her risk tolerance is moderate. She already has $200,000 in her retirement account and is on track to achieve her goals if her portfolio earns an average return of 8 percent. She allocates her assets 70 percent to stocks, 30 percent to bonds.

Mary and Tom are married, 35 years old, and concerned about retirement for themselves and college for their two children, ages 6 and 8. Because these goals have different time horizons, they allocate the assets differently. They want to be more conservative with the college fund, so they allocate 60 percent to bonds and 40 percent to stocks. As the children get closer to college, they will gradually move the money from stocks to bonds to cash. As far as retirement is concerned, Mary and Tom both want to retire in 30 years, but they differ in their risk tolerance: Mary's is high, while Tom's is moderate. Mary allocates 100 percent of her retirement fund to stocks; Tom allocates 75 percent to stocks and 25 percent to bonds.

Diane and Bill are married, 55 years old, and breathing a sigh of relief because their big family expenses—college and weddings—are behind them. Their major financial goal is retirement in 10 years. Since they were late getting started saving, they want to make up for it by contributing as much as possible to their retirement plans and after-tax investment accounts over the next 10 years and maximizing investment returns as much as possible. They allocate 80 percent of their portfolio to stocks and 20 percent to bonds. They understand that this strategy is aggressive for someone so close to retirement and are prepared to see their portfolio fluctuate in value. They are also prepared to defer retirement by a few years or work part-time during retirement if they have to. However, they see this as their only chance to retire with the income they desire.

Sue and George are married, 65 years old, and in the first year of retirement. Social Security provides about one-third of the income they need to live, so they start taking monthly withdrawals from their retirement fund. They shift their allocation from 60 percent stocks, 40 percent bonds to the reverse: 40 percent stocks and 60 percent bonds. This allocation provides the income and stability they need while allowing the portfolio to grow in order to accommodate rising income needs in the future.

STOP HERE TO KEEP IT SIMPLE

If you're just starting out and want to keep your investing simple, you can use this stock/bond allocation to start investing while you learn about the finer points of asset allocation as discussed in the following paragraphs. Chapter 8 shows which kinds of mutual funds to buy if you know your stock/bond allocation but do not wish to deal with understanding the various subsegments of the market. Or, if you're so boggled by all this stock/bond, growth/income business, you can take the really easy way out and invest in an asset allocation mutual fund, also called a *life cycle* (or *lifestyle*) *fund*.

Life cycle funds take into account your age, risk tolerance, and time horizon and allocate assets between stocks and bonds according to what is deemed best for you, in a manner similar to the previous examples. If you wanted to stop reading this book and never again have to think about stocks and bonds and not feel guilty about neglecting your investments because all this financial stuff *simply doesn't interest you*, find yourself a good life cycle fund, put all your money into it, and get on with your life. Later, you may decide to take an interest in your portfolio and learn how to fine-tune it according to steps 2 and 3. In the meantime, don't let your lack of interest in investments paralyze you and keep you from saving and investing. Life cycle funds are made for people like you (and believe me, there are plenty of you). Chapter 8 gives another alternative.

KEEP GOING TO FINE-TUNE YOUR ALLOCATION PLAN

As you read on, you'll see that we are attempting to fine-tune the portfolio by adjusting the allocation among the various subsegments of the two major asset classes, stocks and bonds. All the segments of the market are covered because you never know which segments will be the top performers, so you want to spread your money around. It's like driving on the freeway or expressway. When you're having a bad day, you find yourself in the slow lane while cars in the other lanes are whizzing past you. Then you switch into one of the faster lanes only to have that one slow down. If you're having a really bad day, a stalled vehicle in your lane stops you dead in your tracks. Investing across many segments of the markets is like having a car in every lane; some speed up while others slow down. Everybody gets there eventually, just at different times (except for the poor car that had to be towed to the shop; that's what can happen when you invest in risky stocks).

Step Two: Divide the Stock Portion of the Portfolio

There are three ways to slice up the stock portion of your portfolio: growth stocks versus value stocks, large companies versus small companies, and domestic versus international.

1. Growth versus value.

Growth stocks are companies in rapidly growing industries, have rapidly growing sales, and, hopefully, rapidly growing earnings. The advantage of investing in growth stocks is that as a company's earnings increase, the stock price should increase. And since a company's earnings potential is virtually unlimited, the potential of its stock price is virtually unlimited. The disadvantage is that if the earnings don't grow as much as investors expect, the stock price may not go up very much at all because these stocks are usually priced pretty high to begin with. Value stocks are considered bargains. They're out of favor with Wall Street and are in the doldrums. In some cases the problem is specific to the company; perhaps it has had major financial difficulties or even filed bankruptcy. In other cases an entire industry is out of favor due to a lull in the business cycle. In either case, their stock prices are cheap, especially compared to growth stocks. The theory is that value stocks will come back if given enough time. Whereas growth

stock investors are willing to pay a lot for a company with growing earnings, value investors believe that as long as the price is
right the stock can't help but go up if given enough time. This
doesn't always happen, of course; sometimes growth stocks
don't grow as expected and value stocks are priced low because
they have little to offer. What's important from an asset allocation
standpoint is that these two segments of the market usually perform opposite to each other: When growth stocks are in favor,
value stocks are out of favor and vice versa. During the technology boom of the 1990s, value stocks weren't very popular. But as
growth companies' earnings have slowed down more recently,
investors are starting to look for bargains once again.

2. Large companies versus small companies versus mid-size companies.

Another way to apportion stock class is by capitalization. A
stock's capitalization is its share price multiplied by the number
of shares outstanding. Stocks are categorized as large-cap, mid-
cap, and small-cap. These market segments perform differently at
different times. For example, in 1998 large growth stocks were
up 38.7 percent, while small growth stocks were up just 1.2 percent. In 1992, small value stocks were up 29.2 percent while
large value stocks were up just 13.8 percent. And again, because
it's impossible to know which segment is getting ready to be on
top, we spread our money among the segments to make sure we
have them all. It is okay to get fancy with this appointment if you
really want to (but only if you're so inclined; don't feel like you
have to). If you think that small-cap stocks are ready for a run,
you may wish to overweight your portfolio in small stocks relative
to large stocks. This can be dangerous if you don't do it right.
Most people do it by looking at past performance. They see that
large-cap stocks were on top last year so they shift their money
there, just in time for large-caps to take a fall. Successful investors
are always looking ahead; they generally seek out the more un-
popular areas of the market and get in *before* they become popular. The beauty of this asset allocation plan is that you can
fine-tune it as much or as little as you want. You can divide your

money equally among all three capitalization segments, or you can overweight the segment you think will do the best.

3. Domestic versus international.

It's awfully egocentric of us to distinguish between the United States and the whole rest of the world, but there's no denying our nation has been an economic superpower for some time now. Indeed, much of the business going on around the world is generated by U.S.-based multinational corporations. You could consider your investment in many of our nation's largest growth companies as covering both domestic and international markets. However, there are also opportunities to invest in small, local markets in various countries around the world. These international investments are similar to small growth stocks: They offer the potential for large gains but also carry more risk.

When fine-tuning a portfolio, professional advisors generally alter the mix of these different kinds of stocks based on their outlook for the economy and the markets. For example, when the economy is booming and growth stocks are in favor, they will overweight growth stocks and underweight value stocks. In other cases they'll recommend a 50-50 mix. The goal of investing is to strike a good balance between concentration (to take advantage of changing market conditions) and diversification (to hedge your bets). When you're first starting out, you may not have enough knowledge yet to understand the nuances of how these classes will perform. That's okay. Since diversification is the safer route, focus on covering all the subcategories to start. Later, you can shift your money around as you develop a better feel for the markets.

Figure 7-1 will give you an idea of how the various segments of the market have performed each year since 1986. Of particular note is how the positions change from year to year. For example, in 1999 Small Value was the worst-performing segment, down 1.5 percent. The very next year it was the best-performing segment, up 22.80 percent. Hindsight can sometimes be dangerous because it makes you think predicting the market is easy. But one thing hindsight can show is that the natural tendency to follow

Figure 7-1 Changing global market leadership. This chart ranks the best- to worst-performing asset classes per calendar year from top to bottom. Styles go in and out of favor, thus the importance of diversification. *Source:* PSN by Effron Enterprises, Inc.

1986	1987	1988	1989	1990	1991	1992	1993	1994	1995	1996	1997	1998	1999	2000
Int'l 69.9%	Int'l 25.3%	Small Value 29.5%	Large Growth 35.9%	Large Growth -0.3%	Small Growth 51.2%	Small Value 29.2%	Int'l 33.0%	Int'l 8.1%	Large Value 38.4%	Large Growth 23.1%	Large Value 35.2%	Large Growth 38.7%	Mid Growth 51.3%	Small Value 22.83%
Large Value 20.0%	Large Growth 5.3%	Int'l 28.6%	S&P 500 31.7%	S&P 500 -3.2%	Mid Growth 47.0%	Mid Value 21.68%	Small Value 23.9%	Large Growth 2.7%	S&P 500 37.6%	S&P 500 22.9%	Mid Value 34.4%	S&P 500 28.8%	Small Growth 43.1%	Mid Value 19.18%
S&P 500 18.2%	S&P 500 5.2%	Mid Value 24.6%	Mid Growth 31.5%	Mid Growth -5.1%	Small Value 41.7%	Large Value 13.8%	Large Value 18.1%	S&P 500 1.3%	Large Growth 37.2%	Large Value 21.6%	S&P 500 33.4%	Int'l 20.3%	Large Growth 33.2%	Large Value 7.01%
Mid Value 17.9%	Mid Growth 2.8%	Large Value 23.2%	Large Value 25.2%	Large Value -8.1%	Large Growth 41.2%	Mid Growth 8.7%	Mid Value 15.6%	Small Value -1.6%	Mid Value 34.9%	Small Value 21.4%	Small Value 31.8%	Mid Growth 17.9%	Int'l 27.3%	S&P 500 -9.11%
Mid Growth 17.5%	Large Value 0.5%	Small Growth 20.4%	Mid Value 22.7%	Mid Value -16.1%	Mid Value 37.9%	Small Growth 7.8%	Small Growth 13.4%	Large Value -2.0%	Mid Growth 34.0%	Mid Value 20.3%	Large Growth 30.5%	Large Value 15.6%	S&P 500 21%	Mid Growth -11.75%
Large Growth 15.4%	Mid Value -2.2%	S&P 500 16.6%	Small Growth 20.2%	Small Growth -17.4%	S&P 500 30.5%	S&P 500 7.6%	Mid Growth 11.2%	Mid Value -2.1%	Small Value 31.0%	Mid Growth 17.5%	Mid Growth 22.5%	Mid Value 5.1%	Large Value 7.4%	Int'l -13.95%
Small Value 7.4%	Small Value -7.1%	Mid Growth 12.9%	Small Value 12.4%	Small Value -21.8%	Large Value 24.6%	Large Growth 5.0%	S&P 500 10.1%	Mid Growth -2.2%	Small Growth 25.8%	Small Growth 11.3%	Small Growth 13.0%	Small Growth 1.2%	Mid Value -0.1%	Large Growth -22.42%
Small Growth 3.6%	Small Growth -10.5%	Large Growth 11.3%	Int'l 10.8%	Int'l -23.2%	Int'l 12.5%	Int'l -11.8%	Large Growth 2.9%	Small Growth -2.4%	Int'l 11.6%	Int'l 6.4%	Int'l 2.1%	Small Value -6.5%	Small Value -1.5%	Small Growth -22.43%

S&P 500—Capitalization weighted benchmark that tracks broad-based changes in the U.S. market. The index is calculated on a total return basis with dividends reinvested.

Int'l—The EAFE index is a market capitalization index that includes over 1,053 stocks from Europe, Australia, New Zealand, and the Far East (including Japan, which equals approx. 45 percent of the index).

Large Growth—The Russell 1000 Growth contains those securities in the Russell 1000 with a greater-than-average growth orientation.

Large Value—The Russell 1000 Value contains those securities in the Russell 1000 with less-than-average growth orientation.

Mid Growth—The Russell Mid Growth contains those securities in the Russell Mid Cap (a mid-cap index) with greater-than-average growth orientation.

Mid Value—The Russell Mid Value contains those securities in the Russell Mid Cap (a mid-cap index) with less-than-average growth orientation.

Small Growth—The Russell 2000 Growth contains those securities in the Russell 2000 (a small-cap index) with greater-than average growth orientation.

Small Value—The Russell 2000 Value contains those securities in the Russell 2000 (a small-cap index) with less-than-average growth orientation.

the best-performing segment is often the worst thing you can do. By the time it becomes apparent that a particular segment has done well, its run is usually over and the time has come for a different market segment to star.

Allocating by Industry

Some investors like to further subdivide their portfolio by focusing on specific industries. There is good reason for this, as stocks are often subject to what is called *sector rotation*. Based on business cycles and economic events, along with a fair amount of speculation by market participants, market leadership will rotate from technology stocks to financial stocks to health care stocks, and so on. Sometimes these trends last no more than a few weeks. When that's the case, it's useless to try to ride the wave because it takes you that long to figure out what's going on and then leadership shifts again. But if you look at the longer term trends and overweight your portfolio in those industries you think will benefit from these trends, you may be able to increase your rate of return over what you would earn in a more broadly diversified portfolio. Again, it's a matter of striking the right blend of diversification and concentration.

For example, an important societal trend taking place today is the aging of the baby boom generation. As boomers move into their prime investing years (45 to 65), financial services companies should benefit from the increased business. As our looks begin to go and our health begins to fail, health care companies will benefit. Other industries that may come in and out of favor as various societal and economic trends take shape are communications, technology, utilities, and natural resources.

You do not have to allocate your portfolio by industry. By making sure you have the other bases covered—growth/value, large/mid/small, domestic/international—you will automatically be investing in these industries. The portfolio managers of the mutual funds you've chosen (more on funds in Chapter 8) will be surveying the economy and identifying trends. Their research will lead them to the favored industries, and most of them will naturally overweight their portfolios in stocks with good long-term potential. However, if you have definite opinions about specific industries and you want your portfolio to reflect your outlook, you may wish to allocate your assets by industry. This requires much more research and attention, of course, than investing in a diversified fund and letting the portfolio manager do her job.

ALLOCATING INTERNATIONAL STOCKS BY COUNTRY

The world is a pretty big place, and to allocate part of your portfolio to "international" doesn't begin to hone in on which areas of the world are experiencing economic booms. Once again, it's the mutual fund portfolio manager's job to know these things, so by investing in a good international fund you can sit back and let the professionals study foreign business cycles, currency fluctuations, and the various political and economic events that determine investment success around the world. However, if you have opinions about which areas of the world you think are due to shine, you can fine-tune the international portion of your asset allocation plan by allocating percentages to Europe, Latin America, Japan, and so on.

Step Three: Divide the Bond Portion of the Portfolio

There are three ways to slice up the bond portion of your portfolio: by quality, maturity, and tax status.

QUALITY

A bond's quality relates to how creditworthy the issuer is, in other words, how likely the issuer is to make its interest payments and give bondholders back their original principal when the bond matures. From a quality standpoint, bond issuers are usually grouped into two categories: government and corporate. Government bonds (including those issued by the U.S. Treasury as well as agencies of the U.S. government, such as the Government National Mortgage Association, or GNMA) are considered safer than corporate bonds, simply because the government has taxing authority. Theoretically at least, the government will never run out of money because it can always collect more taxes from its citizens. The quality of a corporate bond, however, depends on the fortunes of the individual company issuing the bond. Large, well-established companies are more likely to meet their interest and principal payments than are smaller companies that may be highly leveraged. You can determine the creditworthiness of a corporate bond by checking its rating: from AAA (highest) to C or lower. Why would anybody want to buy a lower quality bond? Because the yield is higher. In the bond world, there's a fairly direct inverse relationship between risk and reward: The higher the quality, the lower the yield and vice versa. Conservative investors tend to stick to high-quality bonds, while more aggressive investors may want to include some lower quality bonds in order to increase their overall yield.

MATURITY

Under normal circumstances, the more years that stand between now and the bond's maturity date, the higher your yield will be. The rationale is that the longer bondholders have to wait to get their principal back, the more bad things could happen to increase the risk. One of the best features of bonds is their predictability: You know exactly how much interest you will receive and you know the exact date on which you will get your principal back (assuming you don't sell prior to maturity). A popular bond strategy is to "ladder" maturities, structuring the portfolio so you have some bonds coming due at, say, 2- or 5-year intervals. This strategy not only diversifies the portfolio and allows you to earn the higher yields available with the longer maturities, it also helps you plan your own spending. It's an especially suitable strategy for college saving. By investing in bonds that mature in the years coinciding with the 4 years of tuition payments, you know the money will be there. For example, if you know your child will start college in September 2015, you can buy bonds that mature in 2015, 2016, 2017, and 2018. As each year's bond comes due, you put the money into a money market fund and write checks out of it for the year's expenses.

TAX STATUS

If all or most of your bond portfolio will be in tax-deferred accounts, such as retirement plans or Section 529 plans, you need not worry about the distinction between taxable and tax-free bonds because you won't be paying taxes on your investment earnings anyway (until you take the money out, and at that time all withdrawals are fully taxable with the exception of Roth IRAs and Section 529 plans). But if you are investing some of your after-tax investment account in bonds and if you are in a high tax bracket, you'll definitely want to consider the after-tax yield of your bonds. This means you may prefer municipal bonds, which are federally tax-free (and most are state tax free if you buy the bonds issued in the state where you live). To see which type of bond is best, you'll need to do a comparison by calculating the after-tax yield of both taxable and tax-free bonds having equivalent quality and maturity for your particular tax bracket.

REASONS FOR FINE-TUNING YOUR PORTFOLIO

How you choose to divide the stock and bond portions of your portfolio will depend on your time horizon, risk tolerance, and outlook for the economy and the markets. For the stock portion, the risk lies in growth, small, and international. In the long run, these types have higher return potential than value, large, and domestic, but even the high-potential-return segments could run into a snag, causing the more conservative segments to outperform them. That's why you want to spread your money around and not have too much in any one segment of the market. On the bond side, the risk lies in lower quality and longer maturities, but again, these riskier investments also offer the potential for higher returns.

If you are totally confused by all this segmentation, don't be. As I said before, you can leave these decisions up to the mutual fund managers. However, there are several reasons why it makes sense to fine-tune your portfolio by allocating assets among the various market segments.

1. It forces you to know where your money is invested.

Some people buy a dozen mutual funds because they know diversification is good, not realizing that all 12 funds invest in large, domestic, growth stocks. This is not diversification. By doing an asset allocation plan that accounts for the major market segments and then looking for mutual funds that cover those segments, you will be sure to have the right kind and amount of diversification.

2. It directs you to the appropriate mutual funds.

Mutual fund portfolio managers tend to specialize in certain market segments. It would be rare for a portfolio manager who specializes in large company stocks to also be an expert in the small-cap market. That's one of the reasons you will seldom find all market segments covered in a single fund. By doing your own asset allocation plan, you can be much more precise in your investing and seek out the best fund for each market segment. When it comes to managing your portfolio, you're the orchestra conductor, responsible for hiring the best talent for each section and deciding which sections will play in what proportions.

3. It gives you more control over your portfolio, if that's what you want.

Determining your own allocation plan allows you to actively manage your portfolio and change your investments based on the outlook for the economy and the markets. You can reduce your allocation to the poorer-performing market segments and move more money into the segments that are doing well. This ability to maneuver among market segments can give you an edge in your quest for high investment returns. It's how successful investors consistently earn more than the market averages.

4. It reduces risk.

A well-honed asset allocation plan using mutual funds spares you much of the risk of investing in individual stocks. It provides the perfect balance between diversification and concentration so you can take advantage of market opportunities without subjecting your money to too much risk. And, it saves you a tremendous amount of time. Asset allocation plans do not need to be adjusted more than once a year—usually less often than that—and once you've chosen your mutual funds you can let the portfolio managers do the intensive research that needs to be done before buying and selling individual stocks and bonds.

CHAPTER EIGHT

MAKING YOUR MONEY WORK FOR YOU, PART III

Making Sense of Mutual Funds

A professional is especially careful to make only small mistakes.

Anonymous

Amateurs hope. Professionals work.

Garson Kanin

MUTUAL FUNDS ARE ONE OF THE BEST VEHICLES for investing in stocks because you get diversification and professional management—two tried-and-true benefits that contribute to real growth of capital over a long time horizon. As you may have discovered, individual stock picking can be very risky; large gains can be wiped out before you know it, forcing you to start all over again and make even more money this time to make up your losses. And it's important to understand this concept of "paper" versus "actual" gains and losses. If you buy a stock at $30 and it goes to $80 and back down to $30, you have made no money. When the stock was at $80 you thought you had made some money; you may in fact have been feeling rather rich. You may even have gone so far as to treat yourself to a new car or other extravagance befitting someone with a healthy stock portfolio. But as the stock plummeted you saw how fleeting such gains can be; they're not real at all unless you sell the stock. And that's what mutual fund portfolio managers do. They actively manage the portfolio by selling profitable stocks and investing the proceeds in other promising opportunities. They convert paper gains to real gains by setting price targets and never falling in love with a stock. (There is a tax issue associated with this practice that doesn't affect retirement accounts but may affect your other investments; more on this in Chapter 9.)

Mutual funds also perform a function most individual investors simply can't do on their own: an adequate job of researching companies and deciding which stocks to buy. If you read your fund literature you'll see what lengths they generally go to to find good stocks: reading hundreds of annual reports, visiting corporate headquarters, understanding the competitive forces operating within a particular industry, and much more. Some fund managers even have PhDs in biotechnology or some other specialized field, entering the fund business after several years of career experience in a particular industry and putting their knowledge to work evaluating the various companies. Most fund managers use a combination of quantitative (numbers crunching) and qualitative (subjective opinion) measures to evaluate stocks. Some managers are clearly better than others, and these, of course, are the ones you want to find. But unless you are prepared to give up your job and make investing your full-time occupation, I strongly urge you to outsource this specialized skill and do your stock investing through mutual funds, especially because it can have a tremendous impact on your total net worth.

FEELING STUPID? YOU'RE NOT ALONE

I find it fascinating (and dismaying) that some corporations expect employees to make decisions affecting their retirement savings after attending a 15-minute seminar on mutual funds. Each fund offered by the plan is given about a 1-minute description, followed by a general discussion of the stock and bond markets and a brief talk about risk and reward. Then the 401(k) signup forms are passed out and employees are expected to know how much of their retirement money they want to go into each fund. "Huh?" is the typical reaction among people who have never in their lives had occasion to tell a stock from a bond, much less a growth stock from a value stock. So most employees choose their funds the way anyone would who is facing one of the most important decisions of their lives. They ask their friends. "Which funds are you choosing?" is the most commonly heard question in the workplace following a 401(k) seminar. "I dunno. What do you think?" is the most common response.

It's hard to blame the corporations for this dilemma. They are prohibited by law from giving specific investment advice to 401(k) participants. Their only obligation is to offer a suitable selection of mutual funds and to provide "education" that will help participants decide for themselves where they want their retire-

ment funds invested. The problem concerning this "education" is
that there is such a huge body of knowledge associated with investing that it's impossible to convey it all in an entire college
course, much less a 15-minute seminar. So most 401(k) participants emerge from these seminars feeling confused and inadequate. They are left with the impression that they should now be
able to make smart investment decisions, when they've really
only acquired enough information to convince them they don't
know very much. The tragic result is that many people put off saving for retirement because they're too perplexed to do anything.
Rather than make a wrong decision they make no decision, except the decision not to participate in the company's retirement
plan. Or they make inappropriate investment choices. A few years
ago, before the stock market was grabbing the headlines, people
tended to put all their savings in the plan's stable value fund
because it was the only investment they could understand. Or
worse, they put it all into their own company's stock, thus having
their life savings, in addition to their weekly paycheck, dependent on the fortunes of a single company. Then when stocks were
sizzling, especially the risky small-cap and technology sectors,
they wanted to put all their money there. Hopefully by now,
things have settled back down and people have a more balanced
view of the investment world.

Do not opt out of the plan because you're not sure what to
do with the money. Failing to save for retirement because you
can't decide where to invest is like not eating dinner because
you can't decide what to have. *Any* decision is better than no decision. So ask your friends, throw darts, consult your astrological
chart, anything . . . just don't opt out of the plan because you're
afraid of making a wrong choice. And don't feel stupid because
you're not able to grasp investment concepts on the first pass.
Understanding investing is like fitting together the pieces of a jig-
saw puzzle. You may understand a few of the pieces, but until
you can see how the whole puzzle fits together, you won't have
a firm grasp of the subject. That's fine! You can still proceed with
your saving and investing plan by using investment products designed for people like you.

One great investment product for people who don't want to be bothered making the stock/bond asset allocation decision is a good, basic growth and income fund. Other names for these funds are balanced funds, hybrid funds, equity-income funds, stock and bond funds, and total return funds. If you are going to pick just one fund (and decide not to go with a life cycle fund as mentioned in Chapter 7), a growth and income fund should be it, because it will give you a nice balance between stocks and bonds. A typical growth and income fund invests 50 percent to 75 percent of the portfolio in stocks and 25 percent to 50 percent in bonds. The stocks provide the opportunity for growth, the bonds offer income and stability. You will seldom see a growth and income fund at the top of any of the mutual fund performance lists. That's not their goal. In order to achieve extraordinary performance a fund has to place very big bets on certain sectors or individual stocks and be right. Growth and income funds are instead striving for balance—respectable returns and enough diversification that the portfolio is not subject to undue risk. Look at it this way: If your daughter were getting married, would you want her to marry the unsavory character who could offer excitement and thrills, or the responsible accountant who will be there for her day in and day out? If you have to marry just one fund, let it be a growth and income fund.

A growth and income fund is also a good place to start your journey toward investment enlightenment. Let's say you get turned on by all this investment talk and want to seriously increase your knowledge by taking courses, reading books, and following the stock and bond markets. You know you can't absorb it all at once, but eventually you'd like to really fine-tune your portfolio and choose just the right mix of the right kinds of stocks and bonds. Where do you put your money to start? In a good growth and income fund. This will get it growing in a very sensible way while you begin to study the underpinnings of the markets.

The fund itself can provide a big dose of your education. Read the prospectus from cover to cover to see how the fund talks about the markets. Even more useful, read the semiannual reports to see exactly what the fund invests in. First read the portfolio manager's commentary to find out what the markets have been doing, what the manager's investing strategy has been, and what his outlook is for the future. Don't worry if you don't understand everything at first. Eventually, the pieces will fit together and you'll become accustomed to this new language. Then look at the sector breakdown to see how much of the portfolio is invested in each of the various sectors, and try to understand why the fund chose this mix. Take a look at each security. Try to understand why the fund chose it and, if you're so inclined, do your own research so you can find out more about it.

With so many research tools available on the Web, you can look up each of the securities in the portfolio (go to finance. yahoo.com or www.zacks.com) and dig up as much information as you can find about them. In a growth and income fund you may come across some rather obscure securities, such as convertible bonds and preferred stocks. Don't let this stop you. While you may have difficulty finding the exact securities, you can at least bone up on what these terms mean and further increase your investment knowledge. Putting your money into a professionally managed fund and then looking over the shoulder of the portfolio manager is one of the best ways to learn about investing because it has real meaning for you (your own dollars are at stake) and presumably represents the right way to do things (assuming you picked a good fund). This is a much better way to learn than visiting Internet chat rooms or listening to 30-second talking heads on television.

MATCHING MUTUAL FUNDS TO YOUR ASSET ALLOCATION PLAN

One of the reasons people have a hard time picking mutual funds is that the funds go by so many different names. As we've just seen, funds that invest in both stocks and bonds have names ranging from growth and income funds to total return funds. This presents a real dilemma for people who understand the concept of asset allocation as discussed in Chapter 7 and then attempt to implement it by choosing the proper funds for each asset class. Just when you're all set to find some good stock funds that will allow you to allocate, say, 50 percent of your stock portfolio to large cap stocks, 30 percent to mid-caps and 20 percent to small-caps, you run into names like "Venture" and "Select" and "Mercury." How in the world are you supposed to adhere to your asset allocation plan when these fund names tell you absolutely nothing about what's in the portfolio?

Getting past the mutual fund jargon is absolutely essential for managing an investment portfolio on an ongoing basis. If you were to choose mutual funds on name alone, you could easily wind up with all your money in small-cap growth stocks (those funds seem to have the most interesting names). So I'm going to help you decipher the fund language so you can get past the fancy terms and find out all that really matters: *what the fund invests in*. Remember, when you invest in a mutual fund you are investing in a ready-made portfolio of securities. To find out where a particular portfolio fits within your asset allocation plan, you have to know what's in it.

STOCK FUNDS

Stock funds invest primarily in—you guessed it, stocks. Good guess, because most stock funds don't call themselves that. Instead, they have names like these:

Growth funds

Equity funds

Growth equity funds

Capital appreciation funds

Capital growth funds

Aggressive growth funds

Other stock funds have names that more accurately (or not) describe what they invest in, as we'll see.

Diversified Stock Funds

Diversified stock funds deserve a special place in our program, similar to the place reserved for growth and income funds for people who do not want to be bothered with asset allocation. For people who *do* want to determine their own stock/bond mix but don't want to bother with the finer points of growth versus value, large versus small, or domestic versus international, a diversified stock fund covers most of the bases using a mix the portfolio manager thinks is appropriate.

The problem with some diversified stock funds is that they are not truly diversified. A fund that calls itself the XYZ Growth Fund may actually invest only in domestic large-cap growth stocks. If you were to have this as your only stock fund, you would miss out on the value, mid-cap, small-cap, and international segments of the stock market. Another so-called growth fund may invest only in value stocks. You'll have to do some digging to find out where your money will be invested so you turn to your good friend, the prospectus.

Mutual fund prospectuses used to be the most obtuse, un-reader-friendly documents you could imagine. Even if you were highly motivated to read it, you'd likely turn the last page still wondering what it said. But thanks to the Securities and Exchange Commission's (SEC) recent "plain English" initiative, mutual funds are now required to present certain key elements in a way that normal people who aren't lawyers can understand. One of these key features is the investment objective, which won't tell you all you need to know, but it's a start.

In a diversified stock fund, the investment objective as stated in the prospectus may say something like this: "The fund seeks a favorable long-term return, mainly through capital appreciation, primarily from a diversified portfolio of common stocks that present the opportunity for exceptional growth." This is a great way for a fund to describe its objective if it wants to maintain as much flexibility as possible in managing the portfolio. But it doesn't tell you if the fund invests across all segments of the market. To find out more, read the next section of the prospectus about principal strategies.

This section may either tell a lot or a little about how the fund actually invests. Look for the key words relating to the asset classes: growth/value, large/small, domestic/international. If all these segments are mentioned, it's a pretty safe bet that the fund can invest across all market segments and will likely do so as opportunities arise. This type of fund would be perfect for your one diversified stock fund if you decide to go that route. If there seems to be an emphasis on one segment, such as growth stocks, it may mean the fund does not invest in value stocks at all. If that's the case, you'll need to find another fund to represent the value portion of your allocation plan.

To get an even better picture of the portfolio, look at the fund's latest semiannual report. Keep in mind that you're looking at history—the portfolio may have changed by the time you get the report—but at least you can see what kinds of securities the fund actually buys. Some mutual fund managers have been known to do a little end-of-quarter window dressing, to make it appear that the quarter's best-performing stocks had been in the portfolio all along. Still, they can't "dress" the whole portfolio in one fell swoop, so the semiannual report can give you a sense of what kinds of stocks the fund owns.

How Mutual Funds Are Defined

Most stock funds are not the broadly diversified kind that cover all market segments. Instead, they tend to focus on one or more key areas, such as large growth stocks or small value stocks. Matching mutual funds to your asset allocation plan would be easy if all funds stuck to one market segment. Unfortunately, many of them don't. Mutual funds like to show strong performance numbers because that's how they attract and retain investors. They don't like to hold areas of the market that are performing poorly, so if small growth stocks are stuck in the cellar, for example, they may switch into large value stocks if that's where they can earn the highest returns. That may be fine for investors who haven't done an asset allocation plan and who trust the fund managers to always be in the right place at the right time, but it's not good for you if you are counting on this fund for the small growth stock segment of your asset allocation plan. If large value stocks take a turn for the worse, you have double exposure to the segment going down and zero exposure to the one that may be going up.

This switch to another market segment is called *style drift* in the investment industry, and it pits mutual funds against financial advisors all the time. The mutual funds claim their shareholders want to earn the highest returns possible and it's their obligation to seek such returns wherever they can get them. The financial advisors say such shenanigans mess up their clients' asset allocation plans and cause them to be overly concentrated in one area and lacking exposure in another. That's why advisors tend to recommend funds having "style purity"—that is, where the portfolio managers stick to the agreed-upon asset classes even when they're not performing very well. The funds available through your 401(k) plan may or may not fit this description. Certainly, when you are choosing your own funds for your regular investment account, you can take style purity into consideration, calling the fund for more information if the prospectus and semiannual report don't tell you what you need to know.

Another sneaky little thing funds sometimes do is intentionally give themselves a misleading name in order to put themselves into a category that makes their performance look good. For example, a growth fund that has no bonds in it may call itself a growth and income fund in order to be compared to funds whose performances are naturally dragged down by bonds. Growth and income funds seldom turn in spectacular performance; their claim to fame is stability, consistency, and below-average risk. If you see a growth and income fund at the top of the category with performance that far exceeds the rest of the group, take a close look at the portfolio; if you don't see any bonds, it's not a growth and income fund.

Stock mutual funds that invest in one or more market segments can have a variety of names, ranging from XYZ Midcap Value Fund, which tells you exactly where the fund invests, to

Galaxy New Dimensions Fund, which tells you nothing. Fortunately, there's help on the Web. Morningstar (www.morningstar.com) groups mutual funds by market segment, so if you do a search for large growth funds, for example, it will return a list fitting that category. Now, this list is Morningstar's best guess, because many funds do not adhere to one category. Still, Morningstar's screening tool will give you a good start in identifying funds to fit the various segments of your asset allocation plan. Once you've identified the funds fitting the various categories, you can turn to each fund's prospectus and semiannual report to see if it has the style purity you're looking for. Included in Morningstar's information about each fund is a style box that provides a quick look at where the fund invests with regard to market capitalization (large vs. small) and valuation (growth vs. value). However, this style box is based on the *average* stock in the portfolio, essentially forcing the entire portfolio to fit into a category that may not reflect the breadth of its diversification across market sectors. Morningstar's style box can be helpful if you are zeroing in on a particular sector to fill out your asset allocation plan (be sure to follow up by checking the prospectus and semiannual report for style purity), but when searching for a broadly diversified fund, it's better to look at the whole portfolio, so the style box may not help you much.

Morningstar's categories for stock funds are as follows:

DOMESTIC STOCK FUNDS

Domestic stock funds include funds with at least 70 percent of assets in domestic stocks, categorized based on the style and size of the stocks they typically own. Morningstar's categories for domestic stock funds are as follows:

    Large growth

    Large blend (growth and value)

    Large value

    Medium growth

    Medium blend

Medium value
Small growth
Small blend
Small value

SECTOR FUNDS

If you've decided to carry portfolio fine-tuning to the industry sector level, you can find the funds you need using Morningstar's sector categories. The funds in these categories concentrate on the specified sectors. Some funds may further narrow their focus within the field, focusing on wireless, for example, within the communications sector. You'll need to examine each fund to see how broadly diversified or concentrated it is. Sector funds are a great way to place bets on the industries you think will outperform in the coming years without having to identify the winning companies. Some of these industries are exceedingly complex and it takes a real pro to understand market dynamics and where the various competitors fit. This strategy is not without its risks, especially if you do what most people do, which is to switch into a sector just as it's ending a strong run. This is what happened with technology sector funds. Some of them were up over 100 percent in 1999, so people bailed out of their large-cap growth funds to follow the hot sector, getting in just when it peaked in March of 2000. If you're going to invest in sector funds, do it with an eye toward the future, not based on recent performance. Morningstar's sector categories include:

Communications
Financials
Health care
Natural resources
Precious metals
Real estate
Technology
Utilities

INTERNATIONAL STOCK FUNDS

If you've decided to carry your international allocation to the country level, you can find funds that invest in the countries you're looking for using Morningstar's international stock fund categories as shown in the following list. These stock funds have invested 40 percent or more of their equity holdings in foreign stocks.

Europe: at least 75 percent of stocks invested in Europe.

Japan: at least 75 percent of stocks invested in Japan.

Latin America: at least 75 percent of stocks invested in Latin America.

Diversified Pacific: at least 65 percent of stocks invested in Pacific countries, with at least an additional 10 percent of stocks invested in Japan.

Asia/Pacific ex-Japan: At least 75 percent of stocks invested in Pacific countries, with less than 10 percent of stocks invested in Japan.

Diversified Emerging Markets: at least 50 percent of stocks invested in emerging markets.

Foreign: an international fund having no more than 10 percent of stocks invested in the United States.

World: an international fund having more than 10 percent of stocks invested in the United States.

International Hybrid: used for funds with stock holdings of greater than 20 percent but less than 70 percent of the portfolio where 40 percent of the stocks and bonds are foreign.

BOND FUNDS

When it comes to investing in mutual funds versus individual securities, the case for bond funds isn't quite as one-sided as it is for stock funds. There are some very good reasons to do your bond investing through mutual funds and some other good reasons to own individual bonds. It all depends on what you are trying to accomplish and how much money you have to invest. I'll explain the difference.

One of the greatest attributes of bonds is their predictability, especially with regard to maturity. When you buy 10 XYZ 7 percent of 2022, you know that in the year 2022 you'll get your $10,000 back. This knowledge can be very useful for financial planning purposes, as you can key it to college or retirement or some other goal. You also need not worry about your bonds fluctuating in value as interest rates go up and down. You would think of your bonds as you do your house: As long as you don't plan to sell, there's no point in worrying about what it's worth.

Bond mutual funds, however, have no maturity date. The portfolio consists of hundreds of different issues with a broad range of maturity dates. When a bond comes due, or when the portfolio manager decides a particular bond no longer represents the best investment based on market conditions, the bond is sold and replaced with a different one. So if you invest $10,000 in a bond fund, you can't be assured of getting exactly $10,000 back on a specific date, which is a fairly strong case for buying individual bonds instead of bond mutual funds.

However, there's an equally compelling argument on the other side: The bond market is exceedingly complex and very difficult for individual investors to navigate. Bonds are largely institutional securities, purchased and sold in huge blocks for mutual funds, insurance companies, pension funds, and very wealthy investors. Your $10,000 is a pittance in the bond world and would get you only one or two issues because most bonds are sold in lots of $5,000. For this reason, most people can't get adequate diversification with individual bonds. Now, if you choose your bond carefully and make sure it is very high quality, you'll probably be fine. You'll get your interest payments on time and your principal back at maturity, which is what you want. But your yield will naturally be lower than if you were to go up the risk scale a bit, which is where bond mutual funds shine. Because mutual fund portfolios are so broadly diversified, they can invest in those lower-quality, higher-yielding issues and not worry about the risk of default because no single issue comprises a very large portion of the portfolio. The bottom line: You may be able to earn higher returns in a bond mutual fund than with a portfolio of individual bonds.

Another important advantage of bond mutual funds for long-term investors is that you can easily reinvest your interest payments. If you own 10 XYZ 7 percent of 2022, you'll receive $700 a year. You must then find a place to invest the $700 and it may not be at the same rate as your bond. If you wanted to stick with bonds, you would have to put the interest into a money market fund (at a lower rate) until you had enough saved up to buy another bond. However, with a bond mutual fund, you can have the income automatically reinvested back into the fund, where it will be pooled with all the other shareholders' income and invested in longer term bonds paying a higher rate than money market funds.

So what will it be—individual bonds or bond mutual funds? It all depends on your objectives. If ironclad certainty is what you want, buy individual bonds. If you're going for higher yields, buy bond funds. If you're investing for retirement that is many years away, I would recommend bond mutual funds primarily due to the ease of reinvesting the income. Once you retire and have enough assets to build a diversified portfolio of bonds, I would recommend a personal money manager who is expert in evaluating and managing bonds and will keep your portfolio separate (unlike a mutual fund, which is pooled money). This is really the best of all worlds, but it takes most people a while to accumulate enough money to do it.

Bond Fund Terminology

Like stock funds, bond funds also use terminology that can be confusing. Keep in mind that for the bond portion of your portfolio you will be allocating assets primarily by quality and maturity. If you're investing in a retirement fund or other tax-sheltered account, you'll be looking at taxable bond funds because they offer higher yields than tax-free bond funds and the tax break doesn't do you any good in a tax-sheltered account. If you are investing in a regular taxable account *and* you're in a high tax bracket, you'll be applying your quality and maturity considerations to the universe of tax-free funds. Do not automatically lean toward tax-free just because you hate paying taxes. There is a yield differential between taxable and tax-free bonds, and you must factor in your federal and state tax brackets to determine which will give you a higher after-tax return based on what that differential is at the time you are investing.

Diversified Bond Funds

As with the stock portion of your asset allocation plan, you can either invest in one broadly diversified bond fund or find specialized funds that fit the various segments of your plan. If you are investing long term and want a good mix of quality and maturity in order to enhance your total return without undue risk, buy a diversified bond fund and don't worry about "laddering" maturities or allocating by quality. Later on, as you learn more about the bond market, you may wish to fine-tune your allocation plan and diversify in a way that gives you more control. This might involve putting 60 percent in a high-quality bond fund and 40 percent in a high-yield bond fund, for example, rather than letting one portfolio manager determine the mix.

As you start exploring the world of bond funds you'll find names like these:

Income funds

Fixed-income funds

Flexible income funds

Aggressive income funds

High-yield funds

The key words *income* and *yield* distinguish bond funds from stock funds. But like some seemingly diversified stock funds that aren't really diversified, some seemingly diversified bond funds may not be truly diversified but rather specialize in a particular segment of the market. For example, the term *high yield* is usually a tip-off that the fund invests in lower quality (sometimes called "junk") bonds. (For obvious reasons they don't want to call themselves "low quality" bond funds, so it's up to you to know that high yield and low quality go hand in hand.)

Morningstar calls diversified bond funds "multisector" funds. If you're looking for a single diversified bond fund for the whole bond portion of your asset allocation plan, this is a good place to start. Simply ask Morningstar's screening tool to bring up all multisector funds and it will give you a list of all bond funds whose portfolios cross many market sectors. You can also use the screening tool to specify quality and duration, but for your one do-everything bond fund it's probably better not to narrow your search that way because you'll only be reducing the breadth of diversification.

Once the list of funds comes up, you can click on each fund and look at Morningstar's style box. As with the stock funds, this is a quick view of the *average* security in the portfolio; in the case of bonds it is based on quality and duration. (Duration is the weighted maturity of all the securities in the portfolio and is a good indication of how sensitive the portfolio is to changes in interest rates; the longer the duration the more the portfolio will fluctuate as interest rates move up and down.) Again, the style box should serve as a quick look only. For your diversified bond fund you are looking for breadth across market sectors; use the style box only if you wish to lean toward one sector or another.

Specialized Bond Funds

Specialized bond funds focus on specific are as of the band market.

TAXABLE BOND FUNDS

Most bond funds concentrate on a particular market sector, which makes it easy to fulfill your asset allocation plan, as long as you

know how you want to divide your portfolio between high quality and low quality, and between short maturities and long maturities. Here are Morningstar's categories for taxable bond funds:

Long-Term Bond. Corporate and other investment-grade issues with an average maturity of more than 10 years.

Intermediate-Term Bond. Both corporate and government
issues with an average maturity of 4 to 10 years.

Short-Term Bond. Corporate and other investment-grade issues with an average maturity of 1 to 4 years.

Long-Term Government. At least 90 percent of the portfolio
is in government bonds with an average maturity of more
than 10 years.

Intermediate-Term Government. At least 90 percent of the
portfolio is in government bonds with an average maturity
of 4 to 10 years.

Short-Term Government. At least 90 percent of the portfolio
is invested in government issues with an average maturity of
1 to 4 years.

Ultrashort Bond. Corporate and government issues maturing in less than 1 year.

High-Yield. Lower quality and nonrated bonds with average
maturity of more than 10 years.

International Bond. Bonds issued by governments and corporations located outside the United States.

Emerging Markets Bond. Bonds issued by governments of
emerging markets such as Mexico and Brazil.

TAX-FREE BOND FUNDS

If you are investing in a regular taxable account and are in a high
tax bracket, you'll want to turn your attention toward tax-free
funds. As you'll see from the list that follows, there are state-
specific funds as well as national funds that invest all over the
United States. All of them have the name "Municipal" in them
because these funds are made up of municipal bonds, which are

bonds issued by state and local governments and their agencies, the only types of bonds whose interest has been granted tax-free status. My earlier discussion about the pros and cons of investing in bond funds versus individual bonds holds true for tax-free funds as well. For possibly higher returns and ease of reinvestment, go with funds. For predictable maturity dates, go with the individual bonds (but you should have at least $100,000 to get adequate diversification).

When choosing tax-free funds, look first to see if there's a fund for your state. Municipal bond interest is federally tax free for everyone, and it's usually state tax free for the people who live in the state where the bonds are issued. Because there are so many funds for New York and California, Morningstar has separate categories for these. For all the others, look under the single-state category and find your state. If your state does not have an income tax, you don't need to worry and are probably better off going with one of the national funds in order to get broad diversification.

Municipal National Long-Term. A national fund with an average maturity of more than 12 years.

Municipal National Intermediate-Term. A national fund with an average maturity of 5 to 12 years.

Municipal New York Long-Term. At least 80 percent of the fund is in New York municipal bonds with an average maturity of more than 12 years.

Municipal New York Intermediate-Term. At least 80 percent of the fund is in New York municipal bonds with an average maturity of 5 to 12 years.

Municipal California Long-Term. At least 80 percent of the assets are in California municipal bonds with an average maturity of more than 12 years.

Municipal California Intermediate-Term. At least 80 percent of the assets are in California municipal bonds with an average maturity of 5 to 12 years.

Municipal Single-State Long-Term. A single state fund with an average maturity of more than 12 years.

Municipal Single-State Intermediate-Term. A single state fund with an average maturity of 5 to 12 years.

Municipal Bond Short-Term (national and single state). Municipal bonds have an average maturity of less than 5 years.

As you can see from these descriptions, fitting mutual funds to your asset allocation plan is easier with bond funds than with stock funds because bond funds tend to maintain more style purity. If you want to divide your portfolio equally among short-, intermediate-, and long-term bonds, for example, all you have to do is find the funds fitting those descriptions. Or, as noted earlier, just buy one good all-purpose bond fund and let the portfolio manager determine the allocation.

Managed Asset Allocation Funds

Before I discuss evaluating mutual funds, I want to mention another type of hybrid fund that may have a place in your portfolio. A managed (also called *tactical*) asset allocation fund sounds like the life cycle (or lifestyle) funds I talked about earlier, but instead of allocating assets based on your age, risk tolerance, and time horizon, the fund managers change their concentration in stocks, bonds, and cash based on their outlook for the markets. Although these funds may invest in all asset classes, they should not be considered diversified funds because they could go from 100 percent stocks to 100 percent cash if they think the stock market is due for a fall. And that is the reason you might want to invest in one of these funds. Sometimes the stock market goes through periods where it's tough to make money no matter how good a stock picker you are. In those times you want to bide your time in cash. But you also want to be able to get back into stocks before they take off. Needless to say, the performance of these funds depends on the skill and success of the portfolio manager in calling the turns of the markets. Whatever you do, don't try this at home. But if the idea of moving money among asset classes as market conditions change appeals to you, consider one of these managed asset allocation funds.

HOW TO EVALUATE MUTUAL FUNDS

How to pick a mutual fund is a subject near and dear to my heart because most people don't do it right. They place far too much emphasis on annual performance numbers without really understanding how the fund invests. I hope this book impresses upon you the importance of knowing what kinds of securities a fund invests in and matching it to your asset allocation plan. That's the only way to break through the mutual fund jargon and manage your investment portfolio on a long-term basis. Once you've zeroed in on a particular kind of fund, you can then compare performance numbers to see which funds in the category have the best long-term track records. But the last thing you want to do is start with performance or you'll constantly be chasing last year's hot funds (which often turn to ice when a different market sector is on top).

Another mistake people make is choosing their mutual funds the way they choose their movies: using the star system. Now, I would be the first to praise Morningstar for creating a Web site that is an absolute godsend for investors because it presents an incredible amount of information on thousands of funds in an easily accessible format. People especially love their star system because it tells you at a glance which funds Morningstar thinks rank the best in their category, taking into account both returns and risk. But too many people rely too heavily on the star system without considering other factors that can influence fund performance. For example, the tenure and overall industry experience of the portfolio manager can have tremendous bearing on a fund's performance. But fund managers move around. The manager that established a particular five-star fund's excellent performance may not even be there anymore; she may have moved to a fund that is currently ranked only two or three stars. There's an easy way to find this out—the start date of the current portfolio manager is readily available, both on Morningstar's site and in the mutual fund prospectus. The point is that you should not rely on the star system to get out of doing your homework, because there are many qualitative issues that should be considered in addition to Morningstar's quantitative data.

Another big problem with Morningstar's star rating system is that because of the way returns are calculated, it tends to favor the latest hot funds. At year-end 1999, 87 percent of all technology funds had five stars; the rest had four stars. As we now know, year-end 1999 was the worst time to invest in the technology sector. But if you'd followed Morningstar's star rating system and invested only in four- or five-star funds, you could easily have loaded up on these volatile funds which turned out giving back a big portion of their gains in 2000. Funds with long histories will generally fare worse in the rating system compared to a 2-year-old fund that got lucky during its short lifetime. But experience and longevity are what you want when investing in a mutual fund. So please, use Morningstar's Web site for the wealth of information it contains, but don't rely solely on the star rating system when choosing your funds.

Once you've created your asset allocation plan and found a list of funds that invest in each asset class, you can evaluate each fund in the category to make your selection. This procedure applies whether you are fine-tuning down to specific industry for stocks and maturity for bonds or selecting broadly diversified funds that cover all or most of the individual sectors.

Put Past Performance in Perspective

There's no question that past performance can be helpful information. The prospectus tells you how the fund invests, while the performance record tells you how good the fund is at what it does. Or rather, how good the fund *was* at what it *did*. And that's the thing to keep in mind when considering mutual fund performance. It's history. Fund performance should never be used to project future returns, because after you invest, the market environment will be different. Anything a fund did in the past is completely irrelevant with regard to what you can expect in the future.

Where past performance can help is in evaluating the performance of similar funds. If two funds both buy small domestic growth stocks, you can look at their performance records to see which fund did a better job of selecting and managing stocks in that particular market sector. Look at 1-year, 3-year, 5-year, and 10-year records. Look at the start date of the portfolio manager to see how much of that performance the current manager is responsible for. Look at the Principal Strategies section of the prospectus to see how the fund does its research and chooses securities. And finally, understand that luck plays a key part in all of this, especially in the small-cap universe. A manager that got lucky last year may be ending his streak right about the time you come on board.

PAST PERFORMANCE OVER LONG PERIODS

The longer the performance record by the same manager, the more reliable it generally is because it means the manager has found a way to consistently make money for shareholders, with luck having less and less to do with the results. If you are comparing two funds that are similar in all respects, go with the one having the longest performance history.

PAST PERFORMANCE IN DOWN MARKETS

Anybody can make money in a bull market. But markets don't go up forever, and when the markets head south, you want to be in a fund that will protect your capital until the good times start rolling again. That's why it's always a good idea to compare a fund's performance to the standard indexes such as the S&P 500. (Most funds will tell you in the prospectus what their applicable index is.) The ideal fund will beat its index in all market environments—in other words, it will be up more than the index in a rising market and down less than the index in a falling market. But if I had to choose one of those conditions, I would prefer a fund that is down less in falling markets. You have to look for this piece of information, but it's well worth the effort. Not losing money should be everyone's primary investment objective.

Evaluate Manager Tenure and Experience

When it comes right down to it, the person making the day-to-day investment decisions about which stocks and/or bonds to buy and sell is the one who determines how much money you end up with. So find someone who's good at it. All mutual funds must disclose the name and start date of each manager, as well as a biography revealing his or her education and experience. Study this information and seek out funds whose managers have longevity in navigating the stock or bond market as well as other experience that might give them an edge, such as specific industry experience for sector funds. Ideally, you'll want a manager who has been through several market cycles and seen a variety of economic conditions.

Investigate the Clarity of Style/Reputation of Fund Family

There are definite advantages to having all your mutual fund money with one fund family. It makes it easy to move money around from one fund to another as you rebalance your asset allocation plan periodically. (Rebalancing involves restoring your original allocation after market movements cause it to become skewed.) Plus, you gain a familiarity with the fund family's statements, Web site, customer service people, and so on. You never want to go overboard in your loyalty to one fund family, however, because most families have different strengths. XYZ may have a great large-cap growth fund but their bond funds all stink, for example. Still, you can look to the fund family to set overall management policies that will work in your best interests.

Style purity is an important consideration when you are trying to match specific mutual funds to your asset allocation plan. While the fund literature will help you determine style purity, you can never know for sure, because the fund may be dressing up the portfolio twice a year for the semiannual report. Some fund families have a good reputation for maintaining style purity; others don't. When choosing mutual funds for my clients, the reputation of the fund family is near the top of the list. To find out which fund families are respected in the industry, call a few financial advisors and ask them which ones they like.

I hope these two chapters on asset allocation and mutual funds have helped you make sense of investments. My goal is to show you that investing is not as simple as picking a stock that goes up, nor is it so complicated that you must put off investing until you have time to learn it all. By putting your faith in mutual funds, you have full-time professionals navigating the markets on your behalf. By managing your own asset allocation plan, you can be in control without spending a lot of time on your portfolio. And by watching your funds and reading the reports that come to you periodically, you will gradually increase your understanding of investments and become a savvy, confident money manager.

CHAPTER NINE

KEEP MORE OF WHAT YOU EARN

Knowing how to make money and also how to keep it—either of these gifts might make a man rich.

Seneca

The hardest thing in the world to understand is the income tax.

Albert Einstein

INVESTING DOES NOT COME WITHOUT ITS COSTS, which fall into two categories: commissions or fees paid to the financial services industry, and income taxes paid to the government. This chapter discusses both areas and sheds some light on a subject that tends to be underemphasized by the financial services industry and overemphasized by the media.

First, let's talk about investment costs in general. It could be said that no cost is too high if it allows you to earn more than you otherwise would have. This principle explains why people are willing to pay high college costs: A degree definitely increases one's lifetime earning power. It's why some investment newsletters can charge as much as $500 or $1,000 a year: The ads say, "If you get just one good stock idea from our newsletter, you will have paid for the subscription many times over." It's why some money managers can charge high fees and still have very happy clients: The clients are making more money than they ever could have made on their own; even after paying all the fees they are well ahead of the game.

FEES PAID TO THE FINANCIAL SERVICES INDUSTRY

Brokerage Commissions

Investment fees become a problem when you are not aware of what you are paying and therefore have no way of knowing if you are getting your money's worth. Active stock traders often do not take into account the commissions they are paying with every trade. Although they are aware of the brokerage firm's commission schedule and often go to great lengths to find brokers offering deep discounts, they don't think of these costs *at the time they are placing the trades.* It's only afterward, when they get their trade confirmations, that they see how much their trading cost them. And it's usually much later (if ever) that they add up all their commissions for the year to see how much all that frenetic activity cost them. This would be like going to a discount ware-house, filling your basket, and not finding out until after you've been through checkout how much everything cost. Active traders are focused on "points." If they can capture a point on 100 shares of stock, they think they've made $100. But between commissions and taxes, they may end up with half that, or less. And, of course, they have to pay commissions on losing trades as well. In the end, many active traders pay so much in commissions and taxes that they make very little money. Many of them lose money, and often it's the trading costs that put them in the debit column.

The Price of Advice

The financial services industry has traditionally downplayed fees, somehow managing to mix everything together so clients weren't really aware of how much they were paying. Brokers would form close relationships with their clients and recommend trading strategies or mutual funds, and it was almost unheard of for clients to ask how much such strategies or funds were costing them. Implicit in the broker/client relationship was the idea that the costs were irrelevant because the client would be making so much more money as a result of this strategy that it would easily cover any costs involved.

Then in the 1970s the securities industry became deregulated and brokers were free to discount commissions. This was the first time anybody had questioned trading costs because prior to that they had been fixed by the government. Discount broker-age firms popped up, and people who considered themselves do-it-yourself investors, who made their own buy/sell decisions without relying on a broker's advice, moved their accounts to the discounters. Meanwhile, full-service brokerage firms contin-ued to do business as usual. They did not lower their prices to compete with the discounters because they were offering more service: research and advice on investment strategy, dedicated brokers (as opposed to an 800-number customer service line), and lots of personal attention and hand holding. The full-service firms did not worry about losing business to the discounters because they had a very different clientele: one that values personal advice and is willing to pay for it.

Then in the 1980s the media got into the game. Financial magazines proliferated, all purporting to help readers invest their money. One area that was ripe for a little investigative journalism was the amount of fees people were paying on their mutual funds. The biggest revelation to come out of the media's scrutiny of mutual fund fees was the difference between load and no-load funds. *Load* is mutual fund jargon for *sales charge*. It's a fee tacked on to the mutual fund share price, but in a way that's not very visible to the investor. And it goes not to the mutual fund company, but to the broker or advisor who recommends the fund to his client and takes care of the administrative details involved in purchasing it. The magazines suggested that people didn't need to pay these loads and that brokers were somehow being dishonest by having their compensation tied to their recommendations. (The implicit marketing message was that if people kept reading the magazines, they wouldn't need a broker's advice and therefore shouldn't pay the loads.)

Anybody who read the financial magazines got the idea that loads were a rip-off. Why, when there were plenty of no-load funds to choose from, would anybody go to a broker or financial advisor and buy a fund that had a sales charge? The conflict-of-interest aspect was heavily touted in the media, and it was assumed that all brokers were recommending funds and strategies involving the highest possible fees in order to increase their own paychecks. What never got mentioned, but which my clients— bless them—never lost sight of were two things. First, not only do I *not* recommend high-cost funds, I actually look for ways to help clients save fees, by focusing on low-cost funds and taking advantage of breakpoints to reduce their fees even further. (Breakpoints are investment levels at which sales charges become reduced; the more you invest, the less you pay.) My philosophy is this (and it's not that unusual in the investment industry, despite all the rogue brokers you read about): My job is to increase my clients' overall returns, and if it means I make less money from any one client, the fact that I'm doing the right thing will lead to referrals and more business. I'm happy to say that has definitely been the case.

Mutual Fund Expenses

Loads and sales charges relate only to advisor compensation. All mutual funds, regardless of whether they are load or no-load, also have annual expenses that they charge against the portfolio. This means you are paying for them. Do you know how much you're paying? In the dark ages of prospectus history you would've had no idea. But now, you can turn to the section of the prospectus that is clearly labeled "Fees and Expenses" and find out exactly how much the fund charges for things like managers' salaries, marketing expenses, and administrative costs. Morningstar's site also clearly displays fund fees, both sales charges (loads) and annual expense ratios, in percentage terms, such as 1.5 percent. This means the fund skims off 1.5 percent of the portfolio's assets each year to cover operating costs. So a mutual fund that earns, say, 10 percent on the portfolio in a year will return 8.5 percent to shareholders. Or to put it another way, if you've invested $10,000, you're paying the mutual fund $150 a year to manage your money. I'd say this is a bargain, considering the fact that it includes all trading commissions and management expertise. Mutual funds have been faulted of late because as their assets have grown, the total dollar amount of revenues has skyrocketed. Yet the funds have not reduced their expense ratios to account for economies of scale. The uproar and debate within the industry can only be good for investors because it may lead to lower fees.

Does it matter whether the fees you pay are classified as loads or as operating expenses? Not really, as long as you know how much you're paying and what you're getting for your money. For example, mutual fund A shares charge a front-end load (typically 4 percent to 5 percent) but have low operating expenses (example: 0.88 percent). B shares do not have an up-front sales charge, but they do have higher operating expenses (example: 1.55 percent) and also a surrender charge if you redeem your shares within four years (example: 4 percent in the first year, 3 percent in the second year, 2 percent in the third year, 1 percent in the fourth year, 0 thereafter). C shares do not impose a sales charge if you hold your shares at least 13 months, but they also have higher annual operating expenses than A shares (example: 1.55 percent).

So it's quite possible to buy a load fund through a broker and pay lower overall fees than you would pay in a no-load fund with a high annual expense ratio, especially if you buy A shares and hold them for several years. Once you've worked off the up-front load, you're paying significantly lower annual expenses for as long as you own the fund. And since most mutual funds allow you to switch funds within the family without paying another sales charge, you still have investment flexibility. And, of course, when you buy funds through a broker you get advice in other areas of your financial life as well.

Do, however, put the whole expense issue in perspective and don't let a difference of a few tenths of a percentage point determine your fund selection or your decision as to whether to work with a broker. When picking mutual funds you should be focusing on the composition of the portfolio, the long-term performance record, and the experience of the manager. When deciding whether to work with a full-service broker, you should determine your need for an ongoing relationship with a financial advisor. These factors can help you determine investment success, not how much a fund charges for its services. Remember, no cost is too high if you end up with higher returns than you otherwise would have. It's possible to be penny-wise and pound-foolish.

TAXES

Compared to taxes, mutual fund fees are pocket change. Taxes have far greater potential to devastate your net worth if you're not careful. What's one or two percentage points a year in fees when Uncle Sam is skimming as much as 38.6 percent off of every last dollar you make? And if you live in a state that has a state income tax, there goes another few percentage points. Put it all together and you can kiss off nearly half of your investment income to taxes. That's if you fail to plan ahead, of course, which is what this book is all about. Your tax planning must start with a basic understanding of how taxes work. So I will attempt to explain, in the remainder of this chapter, the nature and structure of the United States income tax system. I assume that you have filed a tax return or two in your life and therefore have a basic understanding of how tax deductions work to reduce your taxable income and ultimately reduce the amount of tax you pay.

Understanding Your Marginal Tax Rate

The most important piece of tax information for investors is your *marginal tax rate*, also called your *tax bracket*. This tells what percentage of your last dollar earned will be paid out in taxes. So if you're in the 27 percent tax bracket, for example, and you're contemplating a fully taxable investment, you can calculate your after-tax return by slicing 27 percent off it (plus any applicable state taxes). Then you can compare the result to another investment that may have tax advantages. By always comparing the after-tax results of the various investments, you never lose sight of the open hand of Uncle Sam and can focus on the amount that actually ends up in your pocket. No investment should ever be made for tax purposes only. Willie Nelson and many other famous people have gotten into trouble with the Internal Revenue Service (IRS) for investing in so-called abusive tax shelters whose only purpose was to reduce taxes. The IRS says any such schemes must have an economic benefit, otherwise they're deemed pure tax-avoidance strategies and the taxpayer is liable for back taxes, plus interest and penalties. As long as you stick with our asset allocation plan using mutual funds, you don't have to worry about getting on the wrong side of the IRS (assuming you pay your taxes, of course). But you should be aware of how the different kinds of income are taxed and the special tax considerations of mutual funds.

Let's get back to your marginal tax rate. Table 9-1 shows the marginal tax rates for the year 2001. To find your marginal tax

Table 9-1   2001 Tax Rate Schedule (effective July 1, 2001)

Taxable Income ($)	Marginal Tax Rate (%)
Single	
0 to 6,000	10.0
6,000 to 27,050	15.0
27,050 to 65,550	27.0
65,550 to 136,750	30.0
136,750 to 297,350	35.0
Over 297,350	38.6
Head of Household	
0 to 10,000	10.0
10,000 to 36,250	15.0
36,250 to 93,650	27.0
93,650 to 151,650	30.0
151,650 to 297,350	35.0
Over 297,350	38.6
Married Filing Jointly and Qualifying Widow(er)s	
0 to 12,000	10.0
12,000 to 45,200	15.0
45,200 to 109,250	27.0
109,250 to 166,500	30.0
166,500 to 297,350	35.0
Over 297,350	38.6
Married Filing Separately	
0 to 10,000	10.0
10,000 to 22,600	15.0
22,600 to 54,625	27.0
54,625 to 83,250	30.0
83,250 to 148,675	35.0
Over 148,675	38.6

rate, look up your filing status and income level in the table and run your finger across to the column headed Marginal Tax Rate. This is your tax bracket. It's a good number to know. Don't forget it. Also note the upper income level for your bracket to see how close you are to bumping up against the next tax bracket. This information will do you an enormous amount of good as you make decisions about your investments, your career, and whether you want to remain a citizen of the United States. (Oh, come on, we get a lot for our tax money. Oliver Wendell Holmes put it nicely when he said that taxes buy civilization. Besides paying a lot in taxes is a sure sign you made a lot of money.)

When referring to the table, be sure to use your *taxable* income, not your gross income. To find out what that is, refer to line 39 of your last tax return. Taxable income is what you get after you have subtracted retirement plan contributions and all itemized deductions (or the standard deduction if that's what you use). It should be clear that the more you can claim in retirement plan contributions and tax deductions, the lower your taxable income will be.

Table 9-1 clearly shows the progressive nature of our tax system. Your income is taxed in tiers: 10 percent on the first batch, 15 percent on the second batch, 28 percent on the third batch, and so on. Whenever you are making investment decisions, the assumption is that your decision affects the last dollar of income (presumably all your other income wouldn't change) and is therefore taxed at your highest bracket. This makes tax planning very easy. Just subtract the appropriate percentage from the projected income, and you have your after-tax return. For example, if you invest $10,000 in a taxable bond that pays 7 percent a year, you would receive $700 in taxable income. If you are in the 27 percent tax bracket, you'll end up with $511 after tax. ($700 × .27 = $189, $700 − $189 = $511.) On a $10,000 investment that's the same as a 5.11 percent after-tax return. To find out if you could do better in a tax-free municipal bond, you would compare this 5.11 percent rate to the going rate on munis and buy whichever bond gives you the highest after-tax yield (assuming all other characteristics of the bond are equal, of course).

Tax rate information also comes in handy when contemplating deductions, such as retirement plan contributions. To find out how much you would save in taxes by contributing to a 401(k) plan, just multiply the anticipated contribution times your tax bracket. For example, a $5,000 contribution for someone in the 27 percent tax bracket would save $1,350 in taxes. This effectively reduces your out-of-pocket "cost" to $3,650. I put the word "cost" in quotes because unlike most tax deductions that require you to spend money, retirement plan contributions consist of money you pay to yourself.

Understanding the Different Kinds of Investment Income

The IRS considers your biweekly paycheck ordinary income. I know it's not ordinary to you, but the term *ordinary income* is very significant in tax-speak. Ordinary income is taxed according to the tax rates shown in the Table 9-1, as opposed to some other kinds of income which are taxed at lower rates or not taxed at all. Generally, whenever you hear the term *ordinary income* in connection with an investment, you know that it is fully taxable at your highest rate.

BOND INTEREST

The interest payments you receive from corporate and government bonds is taxable at the federal level as ordinary income. Corporate bond interest is also taxable at the state level, while government bond interest is state tax free. Municipal bond interest is federally tax free and also state tax free if you live in the state where the bond was issued. When investing in fully taxable bonds, be sure to take your combined state and federal income tax brackets into account.

STOCK DIVIDENDS

Stock dividends are taxable as ordinary income in the year they are received.

CAPITAL GAINS

Capital gains income results when you buy a capital asset, such as a stock or bond, and sell it later for a higher price. The income is reported for the year in which the sale takes place. So let's say you buy 100 shares of stock at $20 per share on March 1, 2002. After trading commissions your cost is $2,030 ($2,000 + $30 = $2,030). Now let's say you decide to sell the stock on July 1, 2002, when it is trading at $30. After trading costs your net proceeds are $2,970 ($3,000 – $30 = $2,970). To calculate your capital gain, you would subtract your original cost from your net proceeds: $2,970 – $2,030 = $940. This amount would be reported on Schedule D of your tax return. Since you held the stock less than a year, your gain is taxable as ordinary income at your highest tax bracket. Assuming a 27 percent tax bracket, your net after-tax return on this transaction is $686.20 ($940 × .27 = $253.80. $940 – $263 = $686.20)—not quite the thousand bucks you thought you'd made.

Now let's see what happens if you hold the stock a little longer. Let's say you hold it through all of 2002 and sell it on March 2, 2003. You would have no income to report from this transaction in 2002 (unless the stock pays dividends) because you haven't sold the stock yet. Using the same numbers with regard to cost and net proceeds, you would report the $940 gain in tax year 2003, and pay the tax when you file your return by April 15, 2004. However, in this case it's considered a long-term capital gain because you held the stock longer than a year. Long-term capital gains are taxed at a special rate: 20 percent for anyone in the 27 percent tax bracket or higher, or 10 percent for people in the 15 percent bracket or lower. In this case your after-tax return would be $752 ($940 × .20 = $188. $940 – $188 = $752). By holding the stock more than a year, you saved $75 in taxes and essentially increased your return by that amount. Of course, market movements must also be taken into account when managing an investment portfolio. If the stock is back at $20 on March 2, 2003, you would have no gain at all. I mention this not to encourage short-term trading, but to keep the tax aspect in perspective. Generally, it's better to have long-term capital gains rather than short-term capital gains, especially for people in the higher brackets. But taxes aren't the only thing to consider when investing in securities that fluctuate in value.

A fairly new provision in the capital gains tax law allows you to pay 18 percent tax on assets held more than five years (or 8 percent for people in the 15 percent or lower tax bracket). The 18 percent rate applies only to assets you acquired after 2000.

CAPITAL LOSSES

Want to lose money and feel good about it? Think of your tax bill. Uncle Sam has generously offered to share your pain by letting you deduct some or all of your capital losses from your taxable income. Using the previous example, let's say the stock goes from $20 to $10. You sell it and receive net proceeds (after trading commissions) of $970 ($1,000 – $30 = $970). To calculate your loss, you subtract your net proceeds ($970) from your original investment ($2,030) and see that this little mistake cost you $1,060. Bummer. But look on the bright side. When you tally everything up at the end of the year, you can use this loss to offset other gains (which, it is hoped, you have) and reduce the tax you have to pay on your winners. So if you had another stock that you sold for, say, a $2,000 gain, you could subtract your $1,060 from the $2,000 when figuring your capital gains and losses and come up with a final net gain of $940. If your capital losses exceed your capital gains (double bummer), you can offset up to $3,000 of ordinary income. And if that still doesn't take care of it all (triple bummer), you can carry the loss forward, offsetting future gains or $3,000 in ordinary income for as many years as it takes to work it all off. I hope you never get in this position.

MUTUAL FUND INCOME

In fact, I do not encourage this sort of trading at all except by professional portfolio managers who know what they're doing. And that's why it's important for you to understand the basic concept of taxation: The mutual funds you'll be investing in will be subject to taxes according to the guidelines just discussed. But instead of paying the taxes out of the portfolio, they pass the income through to you, and you pay the tax at your individual tax rate. Throughout the year, the fund receives stock dividends and bond interest from the securities in the portfolio. On a quarterly basis (usually) this income is paid out to shareholders and reported as ordinary income. At the end of the year you (and the IRS) will receive a Form 1099 from the fund stating how much income you received as a shareholder in the fund. Likewise with capital gains: All year long the fund buys and sells stocks and/or bonds. Once a year, usually between October and December, the fund makes a capital gains distribution to shareholders. This income is reported in a similar manner.

You must report the income on your tax return *even if you reinvest the income back into the fund* (very important). If you've elected to have your mutual fund distributions automatically reinvested (which makes sense when you are building wealth), it may not seem like you're receiving any income because you don't recall getting any checks. But for tax purposes you might as well have received an envelope full of cash. The fund will tell you (and the IRS, via the 1099) which kind of income you received, whether it's ordinary income (dividends and interest) or capital gains (long-term or short-term). You are then responsible for entering this information on your tax return.

At the time the fund distributes income, its share price drops by the amount of the distribution. So let's say the share price (also called *net asset value*, or NAV) is $10 at the beginning of the year. As dividends and interest roll into the fund, it gradually increases the fund's net asset value to, say, $10.15. On March 30, the fund pays a distribution of $0.15 per share. When the accumulated dividends and interest are removed from the portfolio, the fund's NAV goes back down to $10. If you are a longtime shareholder, this makes no difference to you as far as the value of your investment is concerned. However, if you come into the fund late in the year, you could be subject to taxes on income that was earned before you got there. This is especially relevant with regard to capital gains distributions, since they are made only once a year. The bottom line: Never invest in a mutual fund after September without calling the fund and finding out when it plans to make its annual capital gains distribution. Once that distribution has been made and the share price has dropped accordingly, you're free to invest.

Some mutual fund managers pay close attention to taxes and try to manage the portfolio for minimal tax impact on investors. Such tax strategies might include buying stocks that don't pay dividends, holding stocks for a long time so as not to trigger a taxable event (this is called *low portfolio turnover*), and offsetting gains with losses. Other managers do not pay much attention to taxes, preferring instead to manage for maximum growth or income, depending on the fund's objective. Morningstar's Web site provides a tax analysis for each fund; you can use this to compare similar funds to see which one has more favorable consequences. Also, mutual funds were recently required to state performance figures on a before- and after-tax basis. This information can be helpful, but it assumes you are in the highest federal tax bracket, which may not be the case, and does not take state taxes into consideration. One advantage to having your own personal money manager who keeps your account segregated is that the portfolio can be managed to suit your individual tax situation. But you need at least $100,000 for that, so we'll return our attention to mutual funds.

Buying and Selling Mutual Funds

In addition to the mutual fund income, you may also receive taxable income from your own mutual fund activity—that is, buying and selling different funds, and even reinvesting the income from your funds. That's right. Every time you receive a mutual fund distribution and have it reinvested back into the fund, you are effectively receiving a check for the distribution and turning around and buying a few more shares of the fund. This is an easy, painless thing to do, and most people let this go on for years without really thinking about it. You check your mutual fund statements every quarter, see that your share balance is increasing, and pat yourself on the back for leaving your investment alone so it can grow. When you finally decide to sell your shares—whether to switch to another fund or to take periodic cash withdrawals—the nightmare begins. Your accountant will want to know the cost basis of the shares you sold so he can calculate the capital gain, and you have no clue what to tell him. If you saved all your statements from day one, you'll be OK because each year-end statement will give the average cost as calculated by the mutual fund company. However, there are other accounting methods that may be more favorable from a tax standpoint. One of them is called *specific identification* where you specify *at the time you sell*, which shares you are selling as identified by purchase date and purchase price. This method enables you to sell your highest-cost shares first in order to minimize taxes. However, you must do this when you sell the shares, not later when your accountant is looking you in the eye.

Tax-Saving Investing Strategies

INVEST AS MUCH AS POSSIBLE IN TAX-DEFERRED ACCOUNTS

If you are doing all of your investing inside a retirement plan, a Section 529 college savings plan, or IRA, you need not concern yourself with tax consequences at all. For these plans, investment income need not be reported as it is earned. This applies both to mutual fund income and capital gains that result from buying and selling funds. The tax consequences come later, when you take the money out. At that time it is taxed as ordinary income at your then-tax bracket (except for Roth IRAs and 529 plans, which are tax free). Even if some of the income you earned in your retirement plan was from capital gains (normally taxable at 20 percent), you'll still pay tax on retirement plan withdrawals at your highest rate, which could be as low as 15 percent, if you're retired and drawing little income. That's actually the premise underlying retirement plans: you defer the tax on investment earnings while you're in a high tax bracket and take withdrawals when you're retired and in a lower bracket. (It doesn't always work out that way, though; some of my clients have done so well in their retirement accounts that they are taking sizable withdrawals in retirement. Still, the tax deferral is always worth it because you get to use the money you would otherwise pay Uncle Sam to earn more investment returns.)

If I haven't said it before, I'll say it now: Invest as much as you can inside tax-sheltered accounts such as retirement plans, IRAs, and Section 529 plans. While it's true that retirement accounts impose penalties for early withdrawals, sometimes it's better to invest there even if you know there's a chance you'll need the money before age 59½. The penalty is only 10 percent, and the tax benefit, if you've enjoyed tax-deferred compounding for at least 5 years, could actually exceed the penalty. Also, there's a provision that allows you to tap your retirement funds early and not pay penalties at all. If you're 55 and retiring from your company you can take withdrawals from your 401(k) plan. Or, if you want to retire earlier than that, you can have your 401(k) money transferred to an IRA rollover account and set up a program of "substantially equal payments" that extend over 5 years or until you reach age 59½, whichever is longer. But don't take my word for this. Talk to your tax advisor for strategies suitable for your own situation, and definitely get help if you opt for the "substantially equal payments" program because it requires precise calculations. The point is that I don't want you to deny yourself the benefits of tax-deferred compounding because you think the early withdrawal penalties are too onerous. You can even take an early distribution from an IRA to buy a first home, making IRAs suitable savings vehicles for young people saving for a down payment.

CAREFULLY MANAGE YOUR WITHDRAWALS

Whether you tap your retirement funds early or let them ride until you actually retire, you will have to pay tax at ordinary income tax rates on any withdrawals you make. This means cashing in your entire 401(k) plan at age 50 is probably not a good idea. To drive this point home, let's say you've accumulated $600,000 in your 401(k) plan, and want to take it all out at once. This action alone would throw you into the highest tax bracket, forcing you to pay tax of $237,600 and leaving just $262,400 in your pocket. But if you withdraw the money over a period of time, you'll likely pay tax at a lower rate, depending on your other income. Retirees who are drawing income from several different accounts, both taxable and tax-deferred (and also tax-free Roth IRA), need to carefully calculate the tax impact of their withdrawals. Generally, retirees draw from taxable accounts first so the tax-deferred accounts can keep growing. But this is not a hard-and-fast rule, and there are other things to consider, so if you're close to retirement you may want to get professional help with this.

BE TAX-SAVVY WHEN INVESTING AFTER-TAX MONEY

After you've contributed as much as you're allowed to tax-deferred accounts, you'll probably want to save additional money in a regular, taxable investment account. Here you need to pay attention to the amount and kind of income you receive. If you are in the 15 percent tax bracket, you probably don't need to get too fancy with tax-saving strategies. But if your bracket is 27 percent or higher, you must never lose sight of the fact that Uncle Sam will be taking a bite out of every bit of taxable investment income you receive. This bite will not interfere with your basic asset allocation plan and mutual fund selection process. However, it may suggest that some funds would go better in your tax-deferred accounts while others, having minimal tax impact, could go into your taxable account. For example, some people invest in bond funds in their tax-deferred accounts and stock funds in their taxable account, because bonds primarily throw off ordinary income, while stocks, if held over a year, generate capital gains. Also, stock funds, if managed carefully, can generate very little taxable income and there are funds that have been designed specifically for this purpose (they are usually called *tax-managed funds*). Again, this is not a hard-and-fast rule. You can invest in bond funds in your taxable account if they're tax-free funds. And it's no sin to earn capital gains in a retirement account and later pay taxes on it at ordinary income tax rates. Once again, tax strategy is only one part of your overall investment planning.

You may also wish to take advantage of another investment product designed for people who have maxed out their tax-deferred savings vehicles and want to defer the tax on the investment income earned with after-tax money. It's called a tax-deferred variable annuity. It works like a mutual fund with what's referred to as an "annuity wrapper." This wrapper is an insurance contract that gives it its tax-deferred status and also throws in some insurance protection to boot: If you die when your account happens to be down in value, your beneficiaries will get no less than your original investment plus a certain minimum rate of return. These products are designed for very long-term savings because they carry early withdrawal penalties if you're under 59½, just like an IRA.

INSURANCE

If you think mutual fund fees and taxes are something, wait until you get hit with a disaster that's not covered by insurance. Also included in the keep-more-of-what-you-earn category are those horrendous events that could wipe out years of careful saving and investing in one fell swoop. Try these, for starters:

- Your good old ex-friend Ray slips on your sidewalk and sues you for $2 million.
- Your dog gets feisty at the park and tears a gash in a little girl's face; her parents sue for $5 million.
- You are named in a class-action suit against an organization on whose board you sit.
- An earthquake/tornado/hurricane/flood destroys your home and most of its contents.
- A neighboring child wanders into your backyard and drowns in your pool.
- The primary breadwinner in your family dies or has a serious accident rendering him or her incapable of earning a living.

Cheery thoughts, aren't they? I doubt if any of these things will happen to you. Still, the odds of any one of them happening are probably better than winning the lottery, so it's a good idea to consider the consequences of such tragic events and prepare for them by buying the proper kind and amount of insurance. Keep in mind that as your net worth builds, you have more to lose. If you get a judgment against you for a million dollars and all you have is $10,000, you can say good luck collecting. But if you have a million dollars, you'll have to pay up. That's why your insurance needs increase as your net worth builds.

When contemplating your insurance needs, you must take off the rose-colored glasses that normally keep you optimistic throughout life and imagine the worst. Become a temporary pessimist and think of all the bad stuff that could possibly happen to you and your family. Then imagine what it would be like to live in the aftermath of each disaster. Chances are, a big, fat insurance check would do wonders to help you cope. Insurance not only provides the money you need to carry on, it saves you from having to deplete your own assets to replace what was lost.

Life

When a working person dies, all the future income of that person suddenly evaporates. In Chapter 3 we used an example of the total lifetime income of a 22-year-old who starts out earning $25,000 a year and receives raises of 5 percent a year. Over his 40-year working career, he will earn a total of $2,992,882. If he saves 10 percent of his income every year and invests it at 8 percent, he'll accumulate another $1,007,555. That's a lot of money to go up in smoke if he meets an untimely death at a young age. Now, if he's single and nobody's depending on his income except for maybe a cat, the loss of income won't matter very much. But if he is supporting dependents, the loss of all that income could be devastating.

There are rules of thumb for determining how much life insurance to buy: generally six or seven times your annual income.

However, I think this shortcut fails to take into account a lot of factors. A better way to determine life insurance needs is to draw up a new budget and a new goal sheet assuming the wage earner is not around. Determine what the shortfall will be without the wage earner's income and multiply it out for as many years as it will take for each member of the family to become self-supporting. (Do this for each member of the family who works and supports the family; also do it for stay-at-home parents whose services would have to be replaced by nannies, maids, etc.)

The first consideration is the children. You've got to get each child to age 18 and then through college. Another big consideration is whether the family will maintain the same standard of living by staying in the same house, continuing with private schools if that's the case now, and so on. And you must take into consideration the needs of the surviving spouse as well as his or her earning potential. If the children are older, the college fund is in place, and the surviving spouse has a good job, you won't need as much insurance as a family with young children and a parent who doesn't work outside the home. I wish I could make all this easy for you, but there's no substitute for sitting down with a pencil and a calculator and figuring out how much money the family would need if any of the adults were to die. Do this every few years, because your insurance needs change as you go through life. It's really during the high-expense family years that a lot of insurance is mandatory. Single people and empty-nesters don't need as much life insurance, if any.

Disability

The only thing worse than a key wage earner dying is when the wage earner has an accident or illness that prohibits him or her from working. That's because the disabled wage earner requires food, clothing, shelter, and possibly help getting around, unlike the dead wage earner whose expenses stopped along with his income. The odds of becoming disabled during the ages of 35 and 65 are greater than the odds of dying, yet many people who carry life insurance neglect to buy disability insurance. And it's not just families that need disability insurance. Single people with no dependents also need it, unless they have someone else they can depend on.

Disability insurance can be expensive, and it doesn't replace all of your income (usually no more than 60 percent). There's a waiting period before benefits begin (at least 90 days), which is one reason to have an emergency fund of 3 to 6 months' living expenses, as we talked about in Chapter 2. Disability insurance policies come with a variety of features, all of which cost money. If you want a short waiting period and lifetime coverage (as opposed to benefits that extend for a limited period of time such as to age 65 or five years), you will pay extra for these and other features. It's up to you to decide how much you want to spend for these extras. A couple of features that are important are cost-of-living adjustments and guaranteed insurability. As your income rises in the years ahead, you'll want to increase your disability coverage accordingly without having to provide evidence of good health. Many employers offer disability insurance. If yours doesn't, or if you think it's inadequate, talk to your insurance agent about buying some on your own.

Health

Most people rely on their employer-sponsored health plan for checkups and the occasional trip to the doctor for various minor ailments. They assume that if something really major were to happen, like cancer or heart disease, the health plan would take care of it. Don't be so sure. Most health plans have lifetime limits. If you need more care than the plan will pay for, your own assets will be at risk. You may not have much choice about which health plan to use, but you should always check the lifetime limits of the plan and consider purchasing an additional major medical policy to cover the really horrible illnesses.

Also be sure to fill in any insurance gaps that may occur when you're changing jobs. The federal law known as COBRA (short for the Consolidated Omnibus Budget Reconciliation Act of 1985) allows you to continue with your employer's health plan for 18 months after you terminate, however, *you* have to pay all the premiums out of your own pocket. This means health insurance that cost you, say $50 per month when your employer was subsidizing most of the premiums, could now cost you $400 or $500 per month. Some people take the risk, letting their old health plan lapse on the assumption that they will quickly find another job that offers a good health plan. This could be dangerous. If your job search takes longer than you expected or you're diagnosed with a serious illness, you could find yourself uninsurable. There's a provision in the federal HIPAA law (Health Insurance Portability and Accountability Act) that says you may not be denied insurance, even if you have a preexisting condition such as diabetes, as long as you have had continuous health care coverage. If you do have a gap in coverage, it may be no longer than 63 days. So if you forgo COBRA and wind up with a 3-month gap in your coverage, you would lose your HIPAA protection when you later decide to buy insurance.

Home

If you need convincing that you should have insurance on your home, just turn on the nightly news. Somewhere in the world there's been a fire, flood, tornado, or earthquake that has destroyed people's homes and all of their contents. Put yourself in their shoes and ask yourself how you would rebuild: Would you have to drain all your savings to start over, or would you stay in a hotel for a little while until the insurance check arrives? The odds of such a disaster happening to you are very slim, and that's why this kind of insurance is relatively inexpensive (except for earthquake insurance in earthquake-prone areas—which, of course, is where you need it).

One rule of thumb for buying insurance of any kind is to consider not so much the odds of something bad happening to you, but the severity of the financial consequences in case it does.

That's why I am focusing here on the really bad stuff like death, cancer, and the total destruction of your home. If your house were robbed and a few electronic items were stolen, you could deal with it (although most home insurance policies automatically insure against theft). But if your house burned to the ground, you'd need serious outside help. Talk to your insurance agent(s) about how much coverage you need in each of these areas, and always weigh the cost of the premiums versus the amount of coverage you get. While you want to be well covered, you don't want to become "insurance poor."

Auto

Most states have laws requiring automobile insurance. And if you are financing the purchase or lease of your car, you have no choice but to carry the amount of insurance required by the lender. Since you probably already have this covered, I won't say too much about car insurance except that the big thing to watch for here is liability. This is the expensive part of car accidents and results when the victim of an accident you caused comes after you for damages to his car, all of his medical bills, and some undefined (but usually large) amount for "pain and suffering." If you have assets to protect, you should get the maximum liability coverage, which is $100,000 per person and $300,000 per accident (100/300). Also consider buying additional liability insurance through an umbrella policy (see next section).

Umbrella

Umbrella policies provide extra liability coverage in case of weird lawsuits, like the ex-friend who slips on your sidewalk and sues you for $2 million. They also cover your defense in the case of frivolous lawsuits; it was reported that President Clinton used a $1 million umbrella policy for his defense in the Paula Jones sexual harassment case. Rich people know that the deeper their pockets, the more likely they are to be the target of a lawsuit, even if it is completely without merit. So as your net worth increases, consider purchasing an umbrella policy for $1 million or more. These policies don't cost very much and are well worth it to protect your assets from unforeseen liability claims.

Long-Term Care

If you're young and vibrant, it's hard to imagine ever needing to go into a nursing home. But you should know that nursing home care is not covered by Medicare and it could be your inheritance that gets wiped out if your parents need long-term care in a nursing home. Long-term care insurance policies are relatively new and somewhat controversial. They're also rather expensive, which is why they're not for everyone. Here are some rules of thumb: First, long-term care insurance generally only makes sense for people over 60. Granted the premiums are lower if you buy a policy when you're young, but if you're too young, you could spend years paying premiums on a policy that could be obsolete by the time you need it. Second, if you have assets under about $200,000, you probably can't afford the insurance, and you don't want to get started paying the premiums (which average $1,700 a year) if you're not sure you can keep it up for the rest of your life. Third, if you have more than $1 million, the portfolio will likely generate enough income to cover nursing home costs without dipping into principal. So it's mainly people over 60 who have assets of between $200,000 and $1 million who are candidates for long-term care insurance.

As we've seen in this chapter, it's just as important to preserve and protect your wealth as it is to build it in the first place. As your assets grow in value, you naturally have more to lose, so you should constantly be paying attention to the things that can chip away at your wealth, such as investment costs, taxes, and the potential disasters that can be covered by insurance. Take a tip from old-money families that seem to have this sense of wealth preservation and protection ingrained in their lineage. They see money as something to be kept in the family and away from the IRS and anybody else who tries to come after it. And they have an army of tax and legal advisors who help them do just that. You may not need all the advisors quite yet, but you can certainly adopt some of their attitudes.

CHAPTER TEN

UNDERSTANDING INVESTMENTS

Your Questions Answered

If you understand everything, you must be misinformed.

Japanese proverb

M OST OF MY WEALTHY CLIENTS UNDERSTAND that the stock market is no place for amateurs. That's why they turn their serious money over to professional portfolio managers and go to Las Vegas when they want to gamble. Still, they like to follow the financial markets and learn the ins and outs of investing, so I am constantly getting questions about concepts and terminology used in the investment business. In this chapter, I answer some of these commonly asked questions.

Although I am including details on the mechanics of stock trading and other nuts-and-bolts information, I would much prefer that you understand the bigger picture rather than clutter your mind with details. That said, the more you know about investments in general, the better position you'll be in to evaluate mutual funds and to be precise in selecting those funds whose portfolios contain investments that are right for you. That way, when you're reading your fund's prospectus and semiannual report, you'll be able to critique the portfolio and decide if these are the types of stocks (and bonds) you want to own.

An important part of building wealth is accumulating the knowledge you will need to manage that wealth. The key words here are "building" and "accumulating." Some people feel frustrated when they first start investing because they are not able to instantly get a handle on it. They'll read a book or two and feel as if they should know everything; when they find out they don't know very much at all, they give up. I have two things to say to such people. First, you'll never know it all. Even longtime professionals are constantly learning, because the markets are always changing, new securities are being created, and new information is always coming out to help investors better understand the markets. Second, you don't need to know it all. As long as you can come up with an asset allocation plan and choose a few good mutual funds, you have all the tools you need to build wealth.

While I would encourage you to expand your investment knowledge as much as you can, rely on the pros if it would mean taking precious time away from work and family to stay on top of the markets. Some people enjoy researching stocks and consider it a hobby. Others have different hobbies and can't be bothered with P/E ratios and limit orders. If you find that some of the following questions fall into the "too much information" category, feel free to skip over them and maintain your focus on the bigger picture. If you're a stock market hobbyist and find some of the following information just too basic, please understand that I am writing for beginning investors, and feel free to skip over the questions you already know the answers to.

What, exactly, are investment returns?

Investment returns can comprise several things: profits from the sale of securities, interest from a bond or savings account, dividends from the ownership of stocks—in other words, all the money that comes to you as a result of investing in a particular investment vehicle.

How do I receive investment returns?

You can usually choose to have investment returns paid directly to you, such as when you own a bond and receive a check for the interest, or reinvested back into the same (or a different) investment vehicle. People who are working to build wealth by investing in mutual funds usually have their investment earnings reinvested back into the funds in order to take advantage of the power of compounding.

How do I calculate my investment returns?

It's always a good idea to calculate your actual investment returns for each calendar year so you can see if you are on track to achieve your goals. The simple way to do it is to take the value of your investment accounts on the last day of the year and subtract the value on the first day of the year, then divide the difference by the value on the first day of the year. Here's an example:

Value on December 31, 2002 $34,500

Value on January 1, 2002   − 31,000

One-year gain $ 3,500

$3,500 ÷ $31,000 = 11.3% return

The process becomes a bit more complicated when you add new money or take withdrawals throughout the year. The following formula isn't perfect because it assumes you are making additions and withdrawals on an even basis throughout the year, but it comes close. Here's an example:

Value on December 31, 2002 (ending balance) $61,000

Value on January 1, 2002 (beginning balance) $50,000

Total contributions made throughout the year $ 6,000

Withdrawals made during the year $ 0

Step 1: Add up all the money you put into the account throughout the year, subtract any money you took out during the same period, and divide by two.

$$($6,000 − $0) ÷ 2 = $3,000$$

Step 2: Add result of Step 1 to beginning balance.

$$$50,000 + $3,000 = $53,000$$

Step 3: Subtract result of Step 1 from ending balance.

$$$61,000 − $3,000 = $58,000$$

Step 4: Divide adjusted ending balance (result of Step 3) by adjusted beginning balance (result of Step 2).

$$$58,000 ÷ $53,000 = 1.094$$

Step 5: To turn the number into a percentage, subtract 1 from the result of Step 4, and multiply the answer by 100.

$$1.094 - 1 \times 100 = 9.4\%$$

Why should I bother calculating investment returns?

It is extremely important to keep track of your investment returns because it can tell you whether you are on track to achieve your goals. You'd be amazed how many people have a distorted perception of their investment returns—either thinking they are doing better than they are because of one great stock, or looking at the dollar amount of gain and thinking it "seems" like a lot (or a little) without calculating the actual percentage return.

What are securities?

Securities is the broad term used to describe all types of stocks and bonds. Technically, a security is any evidence of debt or ownership. This evidence can be in the form of a paper certificate or, more relevant today, an electronic entry in an investor's brokerage account.

What does it mean to own shares of stock?

Owning shares of stock gives you partial ownership in a corporation, theoretically entitling you to a claim on the corporation's earnings and assets in case the company goes out of business. However, most people don't buy stock in companies they think might go out of business, so this theoretical definition isn't very relevant today. Still, it's important to keep in mind that stock ownership is tied to corporate earnings; over time, the more a company earns, the more valuable its shares become. During manias, speculators tend to forget this aspect of stock ownership and count on the greater fool theory to sell their shares for more than they paid. Sensible, long-term investors never forget that they are investing in the future earnings of the company. That's why securities analysts focus their research on determining the amount and quality of corporate earnings, and then comparing those earnings to the current stock price to see if it represents a good value. Both of these elements should be in place—a positive earnings outlook and a reasonable stock price—in order for a stock investment to be successful.

What are earnings?

Earnings are the same as profits. If you take a company's revenues and subtract expenses, what you get is net income, also called earnings. If you see an "N/A" in the earnings column of a stock listing, it means the company's expenses exceed its revenues, therefore it has no profits. If you see a number like $1.10, it refers to *earnings per share*, or EPS, which is calculated by dividing the company's net income by the number of shares outstanding. The EPS is most relevant as a comparison tool to see how the company is doing compared to last quarter or last year. It is the job of analysts to research companies in an attempt to forecast future earnings, which often leads to a projection of the future stock price. For example, the last sentence of an analyst's report might read: "We think XYZ will earn $1.20 a share next year and deserves a multiple of 30; we therefore give it a 12-month price target of $36 per share." (They're not always right, of course.) In the long run, a company's earnings have the biggest impact on the stock price—earnings are basically what investors are buying, after all—but on a day-to-day basis stock prices are affected by many different factors that are often unrelated to earnings.

What is a stock's P/E ratio and what does it mean?

A stock's P/E ratio is simply the stock price divided by the earnings per share. It's also called the *multiple*. If XYZ sells for $30 per share and has earnings of $1.20 per share, its P/E ratio (or multiple) is 25 ($30 ÷ $1.20 = 25). A stock's P/E ratio is a very important indicator of how expensive it is in relation to its earnings. If XYZ were selling at $90 per share, it would have a P/E ratio of 75 ($90 ÷ $1.20 = 75), which is well above the market average of 25. Why do people pay so much for a stock? Because they think the company's earnings will rise. For example, if XYZ's earnings were to triple to $3.60 per share, its $90 share price would be in line with the market because then it would have a P/E ratio of 25. When the market is hot, investors tend to be anticipatory, bidding up the prices of stocks well before the expected earnings have materialized. If the earnings don't come through, or if investors suddenly realize they're paying too much for future earnings that may or may not happen, the stock gets hammered. Needless to say, stocks with high P/E ratios are riskier than stocks with low P/E ratios. However, the best way to evaluate stocks based on their P/E is to compare similar stocks within the same industry. The one with the lower P/E (even if they're both higher than the market average) would be considered the better bargain.

What is a dividend?

A dividend is a reward for being a shareholder. Some of the larger, more established companies share part of their profits with shareholders in the form of dividends. A company that earns, say, $1.80 per share may pay out 50 cents in dividends to shareholders. So if you owned 100 shares, you would receive a check for $12.50 every quarter, or a total of $50 per year. Earlier in the century, the promise of dividends was the main reason to invest in stocks. However, companies and shareholders figured out that if companies reinvested all or most of their earnings instead of paying dividends to shareholders, they could grow even faster, which would make the stock price go up. This appealed to investors who were building wealth for the future. Some people, however, particularly retirees, count on their stock dividends to meet current living expenses. While the dividend yield from stocks is generally much lower than the interest yield from bonds, dividends have one important advantage: They can be, and often are, increased every year. However, dividends are never a sure thing. If a company comes upon hard times it may cut, or even eliminate, its dividend. One way to check for dividend protection is to see what percentage of its earnings the company pays out in dividends. If it's more than 80 percent, the dividend could be in jeopardy if earnings decline.

What happens when a stock splits?

Companies like to keep their stocks affordable for investors, so when the price gets too high, they announce a stock split. The split increases the number of shares and lowers the price. For example, a stock that trades at $100 may do a two-for-one stock split, which doubles the number of shares for current shareholders and cuts the price by half. So instead of owning 100 shares at $100 per share, you would own 200 shares worth $50 per share. The total value would remain $10,000. Although stock splits are really nothing more than accounting procedures, investors do tend to get excited about them because it means the stock is now likely to attract more investors. Over time, stock splits have made people rich. If you had bought 100 shares of Microsoft when it went public in 1986, you would now own 14,400 shares (assuming you didn't succumb to the temptation to take your profits after the second or third split).

Where do stocks trade?

There are two primary stock exchanges today: the New York Stock Exchange (NYSE) and the Nasdaq Stock Market. The NYSE is an auction market where exchange members act as agents for their customers, bringing buyers and sellers together. Trading takes place on the floor of the exchange, located in downtown Manhattan, and only members of the exchange are allowed to be there. When you call your broker to buy a stock, the order is transmitted to the physical post where that stock is traded and matched up with a corresponding sell order. Nasdaq (which evolved from an acronym that stood for National Association of Securities Dealers Automated Quotation system) is a computerized trading system with no physical trading location. Brokers and dealers trading on Nasdaq may, in addition to acting as agents, also act as *principals*, buying and selling stock out of their own inventory. Generally, the nation's larger, more well-established companies trade on the NYSE, while smaller companies trade on the Nasdaq, partly because the NYSE has more stringent listing requirements. However, many companies that could meet NYSE listing requirements prefer to trade on the

Nasdaq. You can learn more about both the Nasdaq and the NYSE by visiting www.nasdaq.com and www.nyse.com.

How are stock prices determined?

By the law of supply and demand. Each stock quote is composed of two prices. The "bid" is the highest price anyone is willing to pay for the stock at that moment in time; the "offer" or "ask" is the lowest price at which anyone is willing to sell. The "last price" is the price at which the stock last traded and is generally determined by the balance of buy orders to sell orders. An abundance of buy orders will push the price up; too many sell orders will push it down. The stock market is like any other free market—real estate, artwork, baseball cards—where buyers and sellers come together. It just happens to be more efficient than most markets because there are so many people trading so many shares of so many different stocks.

What do brokerage firms do?

Brokerage firms act as the intermediary between you, the buyer or seller of shares, and the person on the other side of the transaction who's selling what you're buying or buying what you're selling. Brokerage firms save you from having to call all over the country looking for someone with stock to sell whenever you want to buy some. Sometimes the brokerage firm itself will act as the other party in the transaction, especially if there are no readily available sellers or buyers. If the brokerage firm *makes a market* in the stock you're trading, it maintains its own inventory of stock. It can either sell you the shares you want out of this inventory, or, if you're the one who's selling, buy it from you and add it to the firm's inventory. If you're trading a Nasdaq stock and if the brokerage firm you do business with does not make a market in the stock, your broker will find a dealer that does make a market and buy (or sell) the stock on your behalf. When a broker serves as agent (matching buyer and seller), it charges a commission. When it trades out of its own inventory, it charges a markup. There's not much difference as far as you're concerned; you're simply paying for a service you'd have great difficulty doing on your own. Regardless of how the trade is made, brokers are obligated to get you the best possible price. Of course, brokerage firms do a lot more than execute stock orders. They also help their clients manage their overall financial affairs, including college and retirement planning, and recommending suitable investment products such as mutual funds.

What does it mean to hold stock in "street name"?

It means your stock certificates will not be mailed to you but rather be held by the brokerage firm where you have your account. In the old days, when people held stocks forever and even passed them down to the next generation, it was common to take receipt of stock certificates and keep them in the family safe deposit box. Now, it's easier just to keep them in street name, partly for safekeeping, but also because you can sell them anytime and not have to worry about producing the certificates and obtaining the proper signatures. Stocks held in street name are kept at the brokerage firm's depositary (usually a bank or trust company) and recorded as computer entries. The brokerage firm is listed as the *holder of record*, with you as the *beneficial owner* of the shares.

What if my brokerage firm goes out of business?

If the firm is covered by Securities Investor Protection Corp. (SIPC)— most are—SIPC will either appoint a trustee to liquidate the firm and protect its customers or handle the liquidation itself. SIPC may transfer your assets to another brokerage firm or it may arrange to have your securities sent to you. Keep in mind that your securities and cash are kept at a bank or trust company and are not considered assets of the brokerage firm. If something falls between the cracks in the settlement process, you can file a claim against SIPC for up to $100,000 in cash or $500,000 in securities. Most brokerage firms carry additional insurance on top of these SIPC limits.

What's the difference between a market order and a limit order?

When you tell your broker, "Buy me 100 shares of IBM," you are entering a market order. When you say, "Buy me 100 shares of IBM and don't pay more than $110 per share," you're entering a limit order. A market order will be filled at whatever price the stock is trading at when the order reaches the exchange (which could be different from the price you're quoted). A limit order will be executed only if the stock reaches the limit price. If it doesn't, the order will go unfilled. If the limit order is marked "GTC," (meaning *good till cancelled*), it will remain in force until it is either filled or cancelled. If it is marked "good till ___ [date]", it remains in force until it is either filled or until the specified date. If it is not marked with any cancellation instructions and if it isn't filled on the day it is entered, the order expires at the end of the trading day.

What's a stop order?

A stop order is used to establish a floor under the current trading price below which you do not want to go. For example, if you own a stock that's trading at 30 and you want to limit any loss you may have to three points, you could enter a stop order to sell at 27. As long as the stock trades above 27, the order won't be executed. If it does trade at 27, your stop order will be triggered. Then it becomes a market order and you'll be out on the next trade (which could be lower than 27). If you wanted to be sure of selling at no less than 27, you could enter a stop-limit order with a stop price of 27 and a limit price of 27. However, this does not ensure execution. If the stock is in a freefall and the next trade after 27 is lower, your limit order will not be executed.

What is after-hours trading?

The NYSE and Nasdaq are generally open for trading from 6:30 A.M. to 4:30 P.M. Eastern time, Monday through Friday, except holidays. Some brokers execute orders outside of these hours as a convenience to their clients. However, after-hours trading tends to be light with large spreads between bid and ask prices; it is not a very efficient market.

What is the Dow Jones Industrial Average?

When people talk about "the market," they're often referring to the Dow Jones Industrial Average (DJIA). This widely

watched index is an average of the closing prices of 30 stocks selected by the editors of the *Wall Street Journal* as being repre-
sentative of successful U.S. industrial companies (see Table 10-1).
The DJIA is calculated by adding the closing prices of all 30 stocks
and dividing by a special number, called a *divisor*. When the
DJIA was first formed on May 26, 1896, it comprised 12 stocks.
When the closing prices of all 12 stocks were added up and divided by 12, the result was 40.94. Over the years, whenever a
stock would split or a substitution was made to the index, the divisor was changed to preserve historical continuity. For this reason, the DJIA is always expressed in *points*, not dollars, and it is
useful as a comparison tool only; the numbers don't relate to
anything except as marks on a measuring stick. If the DJIA is at
10,000 today and you know that a year ago it was at 9,000, then
you know the market's basic trend is upward. Many people follow the index to get an idea of the market's general trend. However, it's important to remember that the DJIA comprises just 30
stocks and may not relate very closely to your own portfolio.

What is the S&P 500 Index?

The Standard & Poor's 500 is an index of the 500 largest
companies in the United States as determined by market capitalization (stock price multiplied by number of shares outstanding). Unlike the DJIA, the S&P 500 is a market-weighted index,
which means that companies with large capitalizations have a
bigger influence on changes in the index than do companies with
smaller capitalizations. The DJIA is an unweighted index; this
means higher-priced stocks have a bigger influence on changes
in the index than lower-priced stocks.

What is the Nasdaq Composite Index?

Called "The Nasdaq" for short, the Nasdaq Composite Index
is made up of all the stocks that trade on the Nasdaq Stock Market—more than 5,000 of them. Like the S&P 500, this index is
market-weighted, which means large companies such as Microsoft have a much bigger influence on changes in the index than
do smaller companies. The Nasdaq Composite Index is often
used to gauge the activity of technology stocks, because that's

Table 10-1   The Dow Jones Industrial Average as of 2/20/01

Company Name	Symbol	Price	Weighting[a] Percent
Alcoa Inc.	(AA)	35.58	2.145
American Express Co.	(AXP)	45.59	2.748
AT & T Corp.	(T)	20.69	1.247
Boeing Co.	(BA)	61.59	3.713
Caterpillar Inc.	(CAT)	42.60	2.568
Citigroup Inc.	(C)	52.55	3.168
Coca-Cola Co.	(KO)	60.50	3.647
DuPont Co.	(DD)	42.88	2.585
Eastman Kodak Co.	(EK)	43.43	2.618
Exxon Mobil Corp.	(XOM)	83.95	5.061
General Electric Co.	(GE)	47.90	2.888
General Motors Corp.	(GM)	53.51	3.226
Home Depot Inc.[b]	(HD)	44.65	2.692
Honeywell International Inc.	(HON)	49.30	2.972
Hewlett-Packard Co.	(HWP)	31.07	1.873
International Business Machines Corp.	(IBM)	112.15	6.761
Intel Corp.[b]	(INTC)	32.25	1.944
International Paper Co.	(IP)	36.95	2.227
J.P. Morgan Chase & Co.	(JPM)	50.80	3.062
Johnson & Johnson	(JNJ)	95.51	5.758
McDonald's Corp.	(MCD)	30.68	1.849
Merck & Co.	(MRK)	78.15	4.711
Microsoft Corp.[b]	(MSFT)	56.59	3.406
Minnesota Mining & Manufacturing Co.	(MMM)	113.65	6.852
Philip Morris Cos.	(MO)	48.06	2.897
Procter & Gamble Co.	(PG)	75.15	4.530
SBC Communications Inc.[b]	(SBC)	48.05	2.897
United Technologies Corp.	(UTX)	79.15	4.772
Wal-Mart Stores Inc.	(WMT)	53.87	3.247
Walt Disney Co.	(DIS)	31.98	1.928

[a]The DJIA is an unweighted index, which means that a stock's market capitalization (price times shares outstanding) is not taken into account. Higher-priced stocks have more of an effect on the movement of the index than do lower-priced stocks.

[b]Added to the index 11/1/99.

where most of them trade. When you hear that the Nasdaq was up 86 percent in 1999 or down 39 percent in 2000, this refers to the entire composite index. While the composite is a quick way to gauge the direction of the overall market, it can be very misleading because it says nothing about how individual stocks performed. And again, it may have little to do with your own portfolio.

What are some other popular indexes?

The Russell 2000 is an index of smaller stocks. It was created in 1978 by Frank Russell Company in Tacoma, Washington. First the company compiles a list of the top 3,000 companies as measured by market capitalization. It then slices off the top 1,000 for the Russell 1000. The remaining stocks comprise the Russell 2000. The Wilshire 5000 index is another popular index. Comprised of some 7,000 stocks, it is the broadest market index.

What is volume?

A stock's volume is the number of shares that trade on any given day. It's not unusual for one very active stock to trade as many as 100 million shares in a single day. That's a lot of buyers and sellers! The daily news reports usually give the total volume of shares traded on each of the two exchanges, the NYSE and Nasdaq. Traders look at volume in conjunction with changes in the indexes to get a sense of where the market will go next. High volume always holds more significance than low volume. If the market goes up on high volume, it's usually a good sign; if it goes up on low volume, it doesn't mean very much. Conversely, if it's down on high volume, traders brace themselves for another down day; if it's down on low volume, they tend not to worry.

What is breadth?

Breadth is the number of advancing stocks compared to the number of declining stocks. Compared to the averages (another name for the indexes), breadth is a much better indication of the market as a whole. For example, if today's breadth on the NYSE is 1,214 advancing stocks and 1,886 declining stocks, you know that most stocks were down for the day. This can happen even if the indexes are up, reminding us once again that the DJIA represents only 30 stocks and is not a very good indication of the broader market (or our own portfolio!).

What's the difference between a bull market, a bear market, and a correction?

A bull market is long-term rise in stock prices. A bear market is a long-term decline in stock prices. A correction is a reverse movement within a longer term trend. It's usually used to denote a temporary price decline (up to 10 percent) within a bull market. A decline of 20 percent or more is considered a bear market.

What is the ticker?

The ticker is an electronic display that continuously shows stock trades as they are reported. Each trade shows the stock symbol, the volume, and the price. Volume is omitted if it's a round lot of 100 shares. When larger round lots are traded, the number of round lots is indicated, followed by "s." So a typical ticker display might read: XYZ 4 s 25. This means 400 shares of XYZ traded at $25 per share. In the old days, the ticker was sent by teletype and printed onto paper strips. It was the only way people around the country knew what prices stocks were trading at. With today's computers and the ability to enter a symbol and get an instant quote, the ticker is appreciated more for its entertainment value.

What's an IPO?

IPO stands for initial public offering. When a company goes public—that is, issues shares to the public for the very first time—it hires an investment banking firm whose main job is to find enough investors to buy all the shares. A typical IPO may consist of 10 million shares priced at $12 per share. An offering of this size would give the company $120 million in cash, less the expenses associated with the offering. After the offering is completed, the shares are then traded on the *secondary* market— that is, between buyers and sellers who are matched up by a broker via the NYSE or Nasdaq stock market. After the IPO, the company is pretty much out of the loop until it decides to reenter the capital markets and issue more shares in a *secondary* offering (not to be confused with the secondary *market* on which its shares from the primary *offering* are already trading).

What is momentum?

You know that law of physics about a body in motion staying in motion? Sometimes stock prices go up (or down) simply *because* they've been going up (or down). This is called momentum. Momentum traders pay no attention to earnings or any other fundamental aspect of a company's operations; they simply look for stocks that are going up (or down) and hop in and out very quickly to ride the short-term trend. This game is dangerous, because momentum can reverse itself at any time without warning.

What's a day trader?

A day trader is someone who opens and closes all of her stock positions on the same day. She starts the day with cash and ends the day with cash. In the meantime, she buys and sells, buys and sells, attempting to capture a few cents a share on each transaction. Most day traders lose money, partly because trading costs eat into their profits, and also because it's very hard to pick the direction of a stock on a moment-by-moment basis hundreds of times a day.

What does it mean to short a stock?

The usual way to invest in a stock is to buy shares in the hope of selling them later at a higher price. A short-seller does the opposite: he sells shares he doesn't own in the hope of buying them back later at a lower price. He does this when he thinks the stock will go down. To do this, he must borrow shares from the brokerage firm and pay interest on the "loan" as long as the position is open. When he closes out the position by buying back the shares, it's called *covering his short*. Short selling is dangerous because your losses are theoretically unlimited. When you buy a stock the normal way, the worst that can happen is that it will go to zero. Also, you have the luxury of time: If the stock doesn't move right away, you can hold onto it indefinitely. When shorting a stock, if the market turns against you, you can't hang around too long waiting for the stock to go down, because that may never happen. The stock could keep going on to new highs, creating bigger and bigger losses. And unlike stocks you buy and hold, you can't keep a short position open forever; at some point you will have to buy back the stock so you can return the borrowed shares to the brokerage firm.

What is a margin account?

A margin account lets you borrow money for investing. With a margin account you can buy, say, $10,000 worth of stock and put up only $5,000 in cash. The brokerage firm would put up the remaining $5,000 and carry it as a debit balance on your account. Like any loan, you are charged interest on the debit balance. However, you need not pay off the loan as long as you maintain a minimum amount of equity in the account (this varies depending on which stocks you own and what the brokerage firm's specific requirements are). In an ideal world, your stocks would keep going up by more than the interest you are paying; this is leverage at its best. Leverage at its worst is when the stock plummets to zero and you not only lose your $5,000, but the $5,000 you borrowed. Brokerage firms rarely wait for that to happen. When your equity falls below the firm's minimum requirement you'll get a margin call demanding that you put more money into the account. If you fail to do this, the brokerage firm will, without further notice, sell enough shares to meet the margin call.

What's a 10K?

The 10K is a disclosure document that every public company must file annually with the SEC. It's like an annual report but without the glossy pictures. It tells everything you could ever want to know about the company, including a complete description of the company's business, bios and salaries of the top executives, complete financial statements for the year, and all the risk factors a lawyer can think of. Before the Internet, you had to write to the SEC and wait weeks to receive a 10K. Now you can download them in a flash by going to www.sec.gov or www.freeedgar.com.

What is a proxy?

When you own shares of common stock, you have a right to vote on certain matters concerning the company. No, you can't call up the CEO and tell him you could do a much better job of running the company (well, I suppose you could, but you wouldn't get very far). Matters that typically come up for shareholder approval are proposed members of the board of directors as well as various resolutions. A proxy allows you to vote without having to physically attend the annual stockholders' meeting.

What is a bond?

A bond is a security, like a stock, but instead of evidencing partial *ownership* in a corporation, it is evidence of a *debt*. It's like an I.O.U. When a corporation needs to borrow lots of money, it may turn to the capital markets and issue, say, $100 million worth of bonds. Each bond has several components. The *par value* is the amount borrowed; one bond may have a par value of, say, $1,000. So if you wanted to invest $10,000, you would buy 10 bonds. The corporation would take your $10,000 and use it to expand the business or whatever (you can find out what the corporation intends to do with the money by reading the prospectus). The interest rate is the amount the corporation will pay you every year in interest, say 7 percent. The maturity date is when the corporation will give you back your $10,000, say in 20 years. All of this information is in the bond description, which would be: 10M XYZ 7 percent of 2022. The 10M means ten $1,000 bonds. XYZ refers to the issuing corporation. Seven percent is the interest rate, and 2022 is the maturity date.

How are bond prices determined?

Bonds trade in the secondary market just like stocks do. Once a corporation has completed the offering and received the borrowed money, it will keep paying interest on the bonds to whoever happens to own them. If you were to decide anytime during the 20 years that you'd like to have your $10,000 back, you could sell your bonds in the open market. You probably won't get exactly $10,000, however. The price you get for your bonds depends on the general level of interest rates at the time you sell your bonds. If interest rates have gone up since you bought your bonds—say new bonds with the same quality and maturity as yours are now paying 8 percent—your bonds will be discounted to a price that will make the interest payments equal to 8 percent. So if you are receiving $70 per year per bond, a new buyer would pay you just $875 per bond in order to receive the current rate of 8 percent ($70 ÷ $875 = 8%). It also works the other way. If interest rates go down after you buy your bond, a new investor will have to pay you more than $1,000 per bond to make the interest payments equivalent to the now-lower yield. Just remember this: When interest rates go up bond prices go down, and when interest rates go down bond prices go up. If you hold your bonds to maturity, however, you need not be concerned with interim price fluctuations.

What does it mean when a bond is callable?

It means the issuing corporation can call the bonds in and pay you back your principal prior to the maturity date. Why would a corporation want to do this? To save interest expense if rates go down. Let's say interest rates on corporate bonds go to 5 percent. A corporation wouldn't want to keep paying you 7 percent if it didn't have to. So it could call your series of bonds and issue new ones at 5 percent. Needless to say, this would not be a good deal for you. If interest rates are now at 5 percent, your 7 percent bond should be worth more than $1,000, yet $1,000 is all you'd get from the corporation if your bond were called. And once you get your money back you'll have to reinvest it in the new, lower interest rate environment. Corporations cannot do this at will, however. When a bond is first issued it will state whether it is callable. This is one of the features to look for when buying bonds.

What is a junk bond?

A junk bond is a high-yielding bond issued by a company with a low credit rating. If AAA-rated bonds are yielding 7 percent, a C-rated bond may yield 10 percent or 11 percent. Great yield, more risk. Just one more thing to consider when buying bonds.

What are bond ratings?

Bond ratings are letter grades assigned to bond issues by rating agencies such as Moody's and Standard & Poor's. These letter grades indicate how likely the issuer is to make its interest and principal payments. The highest rating is AAA, which implies nearly zero risk of default. Next is AA, then A, then BBB, then BB, then B, then CCC, and so on. Bonds rated BBB or above are considered investment grade.

What are zero-coupon bonds?

Zero-coupon bonds do not pay zero interest, as the name might imply. Instead, they pay all of the interest at maturity. This means they sell at a deep discount to their face value. For example, you might invest just $3,182 now to get bonds that will pay you $10,000 when they mature in 20 years. This equates to a compound annual interest rate of 5.75 percent. Zero-coupon bonds are excellent financial planning tools because there are no surprises. As long as you hold your bonds to maturity, you know exactly how much you will get back and when. Lots of people use them for college saving. However, they do have one drawback from a tax standpoint: Even though you do not receive the interest until maturity, the IRS taxes you on it every year just as if you had received it. Therefore it's a good idea to invest in zero-coupon bonds in tax-sheltered accounts such as retirement plans, or in the name of a child who is in a low tax bracket. Or, if you're investing in a taxable account, you can buy zero-coupon municipal bonds, whose interest is federally tax-free.

What is the difference between bonds, notes, and bills?

Treasury securities are issued in maturities ranging from three months to 30 years. If the maturity is less than 1 year it's called a Treasury *bill*, if it's 1 to 10 years it's a Treasury *note*, and over 10 years it's a Treasury *bond*. Treasury securities, by the way, work the same as the corporate bonds discussed previously except that the issuer is the U.S. government rather than a corporation. Treasuries are considered the safest of all debt securities because they are backed by the "full faith and credit" of the United States government. Securities issued by *agencies* of the U.S. government, such as Ginnie Mae and Fannie Mae, are next in safety. AAA-rated corporate bonds come next, and then on down the rating scale. These safety ratings, by the way, relate only to the issuer's ability to pay interest and principal. All bonds are subject to price changes as interest rates move up and down.

What is the yield curve?

The yield curve is a graph showing interest rates and bond maturities. The vertical axis is the interest rate; the horizontal axis is the time frame, ranging from 3 months to 30 years. Under normal circumstances, the yield curve slopes gradually upward, showing in graphic form that securities with long maturities carry higher interest rates than those with short maturities. This is called a normal yield curve because under normal circumstances investors who buy long-term bonds would expect to be compensated more for taking on more risk. Sometimes, however, the yield curve becomes inverted, showing short-term rates higher than long-term rates. This situation is unusual and signifies strange things going on in the economy. Professional bond portfolio managers—those running bond mutual funds as well as large institutional portfolios—pay great attention to the yield curve. Their job is to seek out the most favorable risk/return situation at any given time and to actively manage the portfolio to take advantage of disparities and inefficiencies. The yield curve is published every day in the *Wall Street Journal* in the Credit Markets section.

What is the difference between buying a bond outright and investing in a bond mutual fund?

Good question! First, let me point out the basic reasons for investing in a mutual fund as opposed to a portfolio of individual securities. With a mutual fund you get much broader diversification (i.e., more securities in the portfolio) than you could ever obtain on your own without having a million dollars. Second, you get professional management of those securities—experts who spend their days researching stocks and deciding what to buy and sell and when. Third, you get tremendous convenience when it comes to putting money in and taking it out. Mutual funds will accept small amounts, so they're perfect for your monthly savings, and you can even set up an automatic savings plan to have the money transferred from your checking account on a certain day every month. When the time comes to take money out, you can either call the fund and ask them to cut you a check or, after you're retired and taking regular withdrawals, you can set up a systematic withdrawal plan and receive a check a month. These benefits apply to all mutual funds, whether they invest primarily in stocks or bonds or a combination of both.

It's important to understand a key difference between buying bonds outright and investing in bond mutual funds. Individual bonds have a specific maturity date on which you know you will get your money back. Bond mutual funds do not. One reason for investing in bonds is for the certainty that no matter what happens to interest rates during the time you own your bonds, you will always get your full principal back if you hold them to maturity. (This is not the only reason to invest in bonds; sometimes aggressive investors buy them as a short-term play on interest rates.) But because bond mutual funds are dynamic portfolios—as bonds mature, new ones are purchased—the portfolio itself never matures. This means both your income and your principal are subject to fluctuation, which is not necessarily bad, especially if the portfolio manager is skilled in maneuvering the bond market; you may end up with a higher total return than if you had purchased bonds outright. But this fluctuation is something all conservative investors need to be aware of.

Who is Alan Greenspan?

Alan Greenspan is chairman of the Federal Reserve Board. He is often dubbed the second most powerful man in America. Not only do his actions reverberate throughout the U.S. economy in a very real way as he moves interest rates up and down in an attempt to strike an even keel between boom and bust, but his words are taken very seriously. During periods of uncertainty, market participants hang on his every word looking for clues as to what will come next, and they buy or sell stocks and bonds accordingly. But Greenspan is a man of great discretion and he chooses his words carefully. He is highly respected for his attention to vast amounts of data and the care with which he makes decisions. Former Rep. Frank Ikard said of him, "He is the kind of person who knows how many thousands of flat-headed bolts were used in a Chevrolet and what it would do to the national economy if you took out three of them." Greenspan has worked with three presidents, having been appointed by President Reagan 3 months before the stock market crash in 1987. He is currently in his fourth 4-year term, which will end in June 2004.

What does the Federal Reserve Board do?

The seven-member Federal Reserve Board sets monetary policy on such key matters as reserve requirements and other bank regulations, sets the discount rate, tightens or loosens the availability of credit in the economy, and regulates the purchase of securities on margin.

What is the discount rate?

It's the rate the Federal Reserve charges member banks for overnight loans. Although this rate does not affect consumers directly, changes in the discount rate eventually do have an effect on bond interest rates, home loan rates, and other consumer credit rates. Changing the discount rate is one way the Fed attempts to control the U.S. economy. The goal is always moderate economic growth with low inflation.

What do you mean by moderate economic growth?

The U.S. economy is measured by our gross domestic product (GDP), which is the total output of goods and services produced in the United States. Economic growth is measured by changes in the GDP from one quarter (or one year) to the next.

This percentage change tells *if* the economy is growing (depending on whether it's a positive or negative number) and by how much. Investors and economists get nervous when the growth rate is too high because it portends high inflation. They get *very* nervous when it's too low, because it suggests an economic recession. Throughout most of the 1990s we had ideal economic conditions: high (but not too high) growth and low inflation. As we enter the 21st century the economy appears to be slowing and inflation may be heating up, which is the worst of all worlds as far as investors are concerned. In a slowing economy, corporate earnings suffer and this is reflected in lower stock prices. Bondholders suffer from high inflation because their principal is subject to purchasing power risk. What good is it to be assured of getting your $10,000 back in 20 years if it will buy only one-quarter of what it will buy today? I don't mean to issue dire economic warnings, but it is important to understand that throughout your investing lifetime economic conditions will change. You must be prepared to face reality and to move your assets around if necessary.

How is inflation measured?

The official measure of inflation is the consumer price index (CPI), which is a government statistic that can be found (along with many more numbers than you'd ever know what to do with) at www.fedstats.gov. Click on Consumer Price Index in the alphabetical listing and it will take you to a site that features a nifty calculator that measures buying power over the years going back to 1913. For example, something that cost $1 in 1913 would cost $17.69 today. Since the calculator only goes backward, it can't help you project future costs. For that, you'll need a future value calculator, which you can find at www.timevalue.com. You can use this calculator to determine future costs at whatever rate of inflation you want to enter. For example, if a new car costs $20,000 today, and if car prices rise by 4 percent per year, the same car will cost $43,822 in 20 years. If prices rise by 5 percent, the cost will be $53,065. Just another little tool to scare you into saving for the future.

The important thing to understand about inflation is that your own personal basket of goods and services may be very different from the ones the government uses to measure the CPI. What do you care if housing costs are rising if you have a fixed rate mortgage or you're retired and your house is paid off? What good is it to know that inflation is under control at, say, 3 percent when your utility bills are going through the roof and your prescription drug bills are going up all the time? The safest way to play the inflation game is to keep an eye on the CPI for indications about where to invest (most investments do not do well in an inflationary environment; real estate is one that does), but watch your budget to see where inflation is hitting your own pocketbook. This will tell you how to adjust your spending so you can shift from pricey items to lower-cost alternatives.

This chapter has introduced some investment concepts and answered a few commonly asked questions without overburdening you with information you may have no interest in learning. Through the Internet, your local bookstore, and magazine and newspaper subscriptions you can greatly increase your knowledge of investing, and I urge you to consider the time you spend learning an equally important part of your investment program.

EPILOGUE
Proof That It Works

The wise course is to profit from the mistakes of others.

Terence

It is wise to get knowledge and learning from every source—from a sot, a pot, a fool, a winter-mitten, or an old slipper.

Francois Rabelais

IF I DIDN'T HAVE SO MANY SUCCESSFUL CLIENTS, I wouldn't be so sure that the ideas outlined in this book work. By the time my clients come to me, they have already acquired a sum of money— usually through hard work and saving. Some have sold successful businesses and want to invest the proceeds so the money will grow. Others are retiring from their companies and want to do an individual retirement account (IRA) rollover with their lump sum retirement distribution in order to keep the money growing tax-deferred while they start drawing income. Virtually all of my clients understand the long-term benefits of education and train-ing, working hard and carefully managing their careers, saving for the future, and investing wisely.

I wrote this book because there was a short period of time when even my most stable clients got distracted by the action of the market. Whether lured by the talk on CNBC or by their work-place buddies who were buying and selling the latest hot stocks, they decided this asset allocation business was boring. They wanted in on the action. Suddenly, investing lost its appeal as the slow, sure, steady road to riches and became America's hottest pastime. In my mind, it really wasn't investing anymore, but gam-bling. I've never had such a hard time convincing clients that di-versification is another one of those immutable laws that reduces risk and is even *more* valuable when we are experiencing a mar-ket mania like we saw in 1999 and early 2000.

So many of my clients felt they were missing the boat, until I pointed out that they were indeed participating in the market via their mutual funds. If they were enamored of Cisco and Lu-cent (which were soaring for awhile), all they had to do was look at their mutual fund semiannual reports and they'd see that those and many other hot stocks were already in the portfolio (along with many others for balance, of course). For some clients, that was good enough. Others insisted on liquidating some of their mutual funds and taking the money to a discount brokerage firm where they traded hot stocks or took a tip on some obscure Internet companies. One client took 5 percent of his assets (about $50,000) and came back later with $15,000. He thanked me for not letting him take more.

If we could all just see that wealth creation is a lifetime process, with many different components to it, we wouldn't allow ourselves to be so consumed by the periodic manias that threaten to throw us off course. My doctor clients (and other professionals) understand that investing time and money in education and training early in their lives results in millions of dollars in lifetime earnings. My business owner clients understand the value of meeting a need, taking a risk, and working hard to build something that not only provides them with a comfortable salary, but also with an asset that can be sold for a substantial amount of money. Other clients who have been fortunate enough to inherit money understand the need to preserve and protect it and invest it sensibly so it will grow. Here are some examples:

- Larry built a successful medical practice and sold it 7 years ago at age 53. He put the $1,342,316 that was in his corporate pension plan into an IRA rollover and we invested it among several mutual funds. It's now worth $2,398,640.
- Jerry, an electrician, inherited $372,558 nine years ago when his mother died. It's now worth $1,081,000. Jerry is only 44. If his money keeps growing at 8 percent, he'll have $5,325,873 in 20 years. Jerry could retire now if he wanted, but he likes working.
- Justin, a former bank executive, took an early retirement package and invested part of the money in a building. He sold the building and 4 years ago brought the proceeds to me, about $200,000, which is now worth $421,038. Justin has other income to live on, so he takes money out of this account for his extravagances, such as annual vacations. However, he never invades the principal.
- Herb, a consultant who had one extraordinarily successful that which paid him a bonus of $587,054, immediately

invested the money in a tax-deferred annuity. It's now worth $980,000.

- Mary and Bill, a couple with modest income and a commitment to save, have accumulated a total of $199,064 in their various IRA and SEP-IRA accounts, all through small annual contributions and careful investing.

More important than the money is how my clients have managed to maintain very nice lifestyles for themselves and their families, following interesting careers and doing the things they want to do. Here are some examples of clients who are, or could be, in retirement and how they got where they are:

- Bruce, whose father was in the grocery business in Los Angeles in the 1940s, decided in 1965 to buy an empty building and start his own store. Everyone told him not to do it, that it was too risky to start a store from scratch. He did it anyway and the store boomed. In the ensuing years he acquired three more stores, which have also been very successful. Now in his 70s, Bruce still goes to work everyday, even though he could well afford to retire.
- Lawrence, who was an assistant dean at a dental school when his father died, left his position and went into the family business of peppers and pickled goods. The company was in a shambles, so Lawrence quickly learned the business and created a new concept that was very well received in the farming community: He would buy farmers' crops and guarantee them a certain dollar amount per crop. The business is thriving and although Lawrence, who's in his 50s now, could afford to retire, he's afraid to. He'd rather stay with the business awhile longer until he can be sure he'll have enough money to retire in style.
- Howard, a high school graduate, left a good job as a carpet installer to buy a McDonald's franchise in the 1970s. His store did so well that he was offered several more of the coveted stores and at one time owned six McDonald's franchises. One day in 1994 he received an offer that he says was "off the charts." After realizing that he would never

have to work again, he sold five of the stores but kept one in order to stay involved. Howard is another example of a successful business owner who is easing into retirement yet staying involved in the business he knows and loves.

- Valerie is one of those rare people who spent an entire career at one company, got a nice retirement package, and was still young enough to continue to advance in her career. At the age of 49, she received a lump sum distribution of $500,000, which she immediately stashed in an IRA rollover account. She then got a job with a competing company at higher pay. Having a substantial nest egg gives her a great sense of comfort and she now feels she's working because she wants to, not because she has to.

- Sean is doing something unusual today: He's kicking back and truly enjoying retirement. After successfully managing a division of his family's business, he finally sold it for several million dollars and retired while in his 50s. He goes for 2-hour walks on the beach everyday, works out at the gym, meets friends for lunch, is involved in charity work, and loves every minute of his life.

The most important thought I'd like to leave you with is that wealth building is a marathon, not a sprint. It's a lifelong process that requires knowledge, discipline, patience, and the willingness to seek professional help when you need it. It requires you to turn a deaf ear to short-term events that can distract you from your long-term plan, whether it's friends bragging about their stock market gains or (more relevant now) lamenting their losses and vowing never to touch a stock again as long as they live. It's the nature of the markets to be volatile. It's the nature of human beings to follow the crowd. Successful investors are able to ignore the volatility and the herd mentality and stick to the course of action they know works over time.

In the race of the tortoise and the hare, you're the tortoise. What matters is not so much when you get there, but *that* you get there. With patience and a moderate amount of effort you'll make it. Good luck!

GLOSSARY

allocation The process of dividing a portfolio's total assets among several different subsets such as mutual funds, geographic markets, stock sectors, or other subsets selected by the investor. *See also* asset allocation.

annual return The return of a portfolio or mutual fund when adjusted to a per-year basis, typically calculated as a geometric return. The actual calculation can be very complicated, particularly if there have been cash contributions or disbursements. The calculation assumes that the returns for all years are the same.

asset allocation Distribution of investment funds among asset types such as stocks, bonds, or cash among stocks themselves, among sectors, among markets, or among any other subsector chosen by the investor. *See also* allocation.

blue-chip stock A traditional term describing the stock of a high quality company.

bond A long-term debt security issued by a government or corporation that typically pays interest to its owner. *See also* municipal bond.

broker A person who acts as an intermediary between a consumer and a financial service. Stock brokers connect investors to the stock market; insurance brokers match consumers to insurance providers; loan brokers create relationships between borrowers and lenders.

brokerage A company that serves as an intermediary between a consumer and a financial service.

brokerage account An investment account through which securities are bought, held, and sold. So called because traditionally such accounts have been administered by trained securities brokers, agents who access the trading markets on the behalf of individual investors.

COBRA *See* Consolidated Omnibus Budget Reconciliation Act of 1985.

commission Fee charged by a brokerage for the service of assisting in securities transactions. Broker commissions are usually charged on a per-transaction basis; less often they are charged as a per-share calculation or a percentage of assets.

commodity   A good or service—a product.

compound interest   Total interest due by applying the rate to the sum of the capital invested with the interest previously earned and reinvested.

Consolidated Omnibus Budget Reconciliation Act of 1985 (COBRA)   Legislation that allows employee to continue with a previous employer's health plan for 18 months after termination.

day trading   The practice of buying and selling securities (usually stocks) rapidly in an attempt to capitalize on small price movements. Typically, day traders do not hold any stocks overnight. Day trading is a high-pressure and controversial method of investing.

diversification   Owning a variety of different types of investments to reduce risk in the portfolio.

dividends   Payments of profit by a corporation to its shareholders.

Dow Jones Industrial Average   A weighted index of U.S. blue-chip stocks; historically, a very popular measure of the U.S. stock market.

earnings per share (EPS)   A figure arrived at by dividing a company's net income by the number of shares outstanding.

economies of scales   Factors that cause the cost of producing a commodity to decrease as the commodity's output increases.

EPS   *See* earnings per share.

expected return   The amount an investor hopes to earn on the capital used to purchase a particular investment, usually expressed as a percentage of that capital.

401(k)   A retirement plan in which employees elect to defer part of their salary. The deferred amounts are invested and no tax is due on the investment income until withdrawal.

free market   A market where supply and demand are not regulated.

index fund   A mutual fund that has a portfolio designed to simulate the movement of a particular market index.

individual retirement account (IRA)   A popular retirement program authorized by the federal tax code. There are two types: regular IRAs and Roth IRAs.

initial public offering (IPO)   First issuance of stock by a newly public company.

investment banker   A financial intermediary that buys new issues and puts them in smaller packages among investors.

IPO   *See* initial public offering.

IRA   *See* individual retirement account.

large-cap   Short for large-capitalization stocks; a style of portfolio management that emphasizes stocks of larger companies.

liability   A financial obligation, debt, claim, or potential loss.

liquid asset   An asset that is easily salable at a market price.

load   A sales charge levied either when an investor buys or sells a mutual fund. It is based on a percentage of the investor's purchase.

load fund   A fund that requires that investors pay a sales charge or load when they either buy (a front-end load) or sell (a back-end load) the fund.

margin   The amount an investor deposits with a broker when borrowing money from that broker. Margin can be in the form of cash or securities.

margin account   An investing account with an automatic line of credit. Investors may borrow a percentage of the cost of a security from the purchasing brokerage. Doing so is called *buying on margin*, and the brokerage charges interest on the loan, known as *margin rates*.

maturity   The date when the issuer of a bond will repay bondholders a promised amount.

money market account   A deposit account that pays a modest investment return approximately the yield of a Treasury bill. These accounts are partly invested in Treasuries and other kinds of conservative debt.

municipal bond   An obligation of a state or local government agency. The interest paid is generally exempt from federal income tax and sometimes other income tax as well.

mutual fund   An entity meeting a specific set of federal rules and regulations that owns and manages a portfolio consisting of securities including bonds, stocks, or cash for its shareholders.

NASD *See* National Association of Securities Dealers.

National Association of Securities Dealers (NASD) An organization established by securities dealers to regulate the actions of their member firms and brokers as they buy and sell stocks, bonds, mutual funds, and other securities for their customers.

portfolio A collection of investments all owned by the same individual.

prospectus A legal document describing the goals, investment criteria, management criteria, costs, and past performance of a mutual fund, which must be offered to anyone seeking to invest in that fund. Historically these documents have been filled with legalese and have been difficult to read; regulators are encouraging mutual companies to make them more consumer friendly.

risk A term used with many different meanings related to unpredictability; regarding financial activities, the chance that an investor will not achieve the expected outcome. *See also* volatility.

risk aversion The tendency for investors to avoid the risk of losing capital.

Roth IRA An IRA that offers no deductions for contributions but that may provide tax-free withdrawals after five years and at contributor's age of $59\frac{1}{2}$.

S&P 500 *See* Standard & Poor's 500 Index.

SEC *See* Securities and Exchange Commission.

sector A term used to group industries; examples include financials, energy, and technology.

Securities and Exchange Commission (SEC) The federal agency that regulates trading in stocks, bonds, mutual funds, and so on.

SEP *See* simplified employee pension.

share A certificate representing one unit of ownership in a corporation, mutual fund, or limited partnership.

simplified employee pension (SEP) A tax-deferred retirement plan requiring little paper work

Standard & Poor's 500 Index (S&P 500) A broad market index that includes stocks of 500 of the largest companies in the United States.

stock A negotiable security indicating ownership of a company.

stock options The rights to acquire common stock at a given price during a present time period.

style   The bias of a mutual fund or its manager, or of an individual investor to hold stocks of a certain type such as those of large companies, midsize companies, small companies, companies that appear to be good values based on their price ratios, or companies that appear to be candidates for strong future growth.

vesting   The process by which employees acquire eligibility to receive retirement benefits by working for a company for a certain length of time.

volatility   The up-and-down movement of the price of an investment or a market, often equated with risk and used interchangeably with that term.

Wall Street   A colloquial term used to refer to the U.S. stock market and all the involved institutions.

yield   The periodic cash return on an investment: interest on a bond or a dividend on a stock.

INDEX